This graphic story does more than tell us about how God works in desperate circumstances. It helps us to understand how the God of history is using events to accomplish his purposes, not just for nations but also for the individuals in them. This is a must read!

Peter Brierley
Executive Director, Christian Research

'Take my life and let it be, Consecrated, Lord to thee' are two lines from a hymn which Brenda describes in her book as beautiful. She and her husband Lionel have certainly put this into practice as they worked among refugees from South East Asia. I was in tears by the time I had read three pages and found the rest compelling reading and humbling to see what God can do with lives consecrated to him.

Fiona Castle

To meet Brenda Sloggett is not immediately to be impressed by someone who has become familiar with handling hostile, armour-plated cockroaches with a shoe in her hand in South East Asia countries, or fighting with dilapidated sanitation which either doesn't work or has a mind of its own. English village life with its gentle predictability might seem more appropriate.

However, to read *Voice in the Night* is to become aware of an able, articulate, well-disciplined wife, mother and grandmother who has been gripped radically by the Word of God with its intrusive demands and vibrant truth.

Voice in the Night is an autobiographical account of literally taking God at His word. For some, obedience to God's Word is presented as a romantic, idealistic, trouble-free triumphalism. Not so here! Weariness, sickness and exhaustion physically; pressure, confusion and pain mentally; adjustment, acceptance and loneliness socially; trauma, turbulence and draining emotionally; stretching, responding and releasing financially; believing, trusting and demanding spiritually; are all part of the journey. Inner feelings are revealed but the life of faith and obedience has to be lived nevertheless. Political systems need to be challenged. Human bureaucracy needs to be persistently confronted. Bullying and disregard for human dignity needs to be resisted.

This is a record of an ordinary woman often doing ordinary things in an extraordinary way by the power of the Holy Spirit.

Jim Graham

If you have ever asked the question, 'What can I do for the Lord?' with an air of resignation that suggests you can't think of anything, this book will be an encouragement and challenge to you. God led Brenda from a background of legalistic bondage to a life of liberating self-giving for him. It is wonderful to see how an 'ordinary' housewife can be used by an 'extraordinary' God to be a blessing to so many. Brenda needed only two things to embark on this adventure – an openness to listen and discern God's voice and a supportive and encouraging husband. Praise the Lord that she had both.

It would be a great pity if your response to reading this book was, 'Well done, Brenda!' A more appropriate response would be, 'Lord, if you can use Brenda, what about me?'

Stewart Moulds
UK Director, WEC International

Voice in
the Night

Brenda Sloggett

Christian Focus

DEDICATION

For Lionel, Rosemary and Alison, without whose support there would have been no story to tell.

Note: In chapters 9 and 10 Mr. Kong is not the individual's real name and some of his details have been changed.

© Brenda Sloggett
ISBN 185792 577 7

Published in 2000
by Christian Focus Publications, Geanies House, Fearn,
Ross-shire, IV20 1TW, Great Britain

Cover design by Owen Daily

Contents

FOREWORD by Stephen Gaukroger 7

PREFACE 9

1. AUGUST 11th 1956
DEATH'S DARK VALLEY 13

2. LIFE IN FREEDOM 29

3. NEW FAMILY 40

4. UNEXPECTED ARRIVALS 53

5. EVERY NEED SUPPLIED 69

6. A HORNETS' NEST IN RANGOON 85

7. OPPOSITION 107

8. JOY AND SADNESS 116

9. A FEARFUL FRACAS 128

10. RESTORATION AND
A NARROW ESCAPE 135

11. NEW DIRECTION 156

12. CAMBODIA. 166

13. LIVING IN FEAR 185

14. DEFEAT AND RE-DEDICATION......... 197

15. THE WAY OF THE CROSS
IN VIETNAM... 208

16. A CALL FROM KUALA LUMPUR 222

17. NEW HOPE FOR CAMBODIA 232

EPILOGUE 245

THE NEW MILLENNIUM
FOR CAMBODIA 249

FOREWORD

Stories can have a great influence in our lives! From the childhood stories of Enid Blyton, through the adventures of C S Lewis, to the stories of adulthood, a good story can shape our thinking and challenge us to action, as almost nothing else can.

True stories can have even more impact. It is easy to imagine that the days of Christian heroes remain in the past – women and men who were passionately concerned that people heard the good news about Jesus – not only in their own country but also all over the world.

Of course the story of Jesus is 'the greatest story ever told'. In this millennium year his story takes on an even more obvious importance. Two thousand years since the God man came to earth to give himself for the whole world. This book explores one small part of God's world – the connection between this country and South East Asia. It encourages us to look beyond the narrow and often parochial concerns of everyday life to people living in a culture, speaking a language and enjoying a climate of which most of us know very little. This thrilling tale demonstrates how the gospel does reach across all the very human barriers, which separates nation from nation and continent from continent. As you read these pages it's my prayer that you will be encouraged to go, to give and to pray that the good news of the gospel may spread all over the world.

Stephen Gaukroger

PREFACE

Several years ago I had an operation which was not a success. In the three months of enforced rest that followed, I had time to reflect on what the Lord had done in our lives and to write an account of God's great goodness to us over many years and through many dangers. My uncle, the late Mr. Joseph Woodcock of Ipswich, greatly encouraged me to write this book and even suggested someone who might type it. I wish to thank Muriel Gooderham of Ipswich, who typed the original manuscript. When I read it later I was not satisfied with what I had written as the story was about a task that was then still incomplete. I shelved it, thinking that my daughters and granddaughters might read it one day.

In 1998 we were privileged to have many missionaries and valued servants of the Lord staying with us in our home. Each of these much loved friends asked if I had ever written a book and challenged me to have my story published in order to strengthen other people's faith. Because I believe that in these difficult days it is essential that we encourage one another in the service of Christ, I retrieved the old manuscript and brought it up to date. As I have no office skills, my husband, Lionel, spent weeks putting it on to computer. I wish to thank him most sincerely, not just for his work on the manuscript, but for his support throughout. Without him I could not have accomplished all the Lord gave me to do. Working on it together brought back afresh the wonder of God's ways with us and his unfailing provision in every situation we met.

Lionel and I are two ordinary people who have sought to be faithful to the Lord. And if any reader thinks that is either a soft option or deadly boring, I pray that as they read the account of our walk with God their eyes might be opened. It has been hard work and it has been exciting. At times we have struggled and from time to time we have failed, but there has been One who has walked with us, held us together, picked us up and restored us. When earthly fathers fail, we have One in heaven who leads, guides, loves and cares with a depth of understanding that far exceeds our wildest dreams.

Cambodia was the country we were called to help, and our involvement, and this account, only pricks the surface of the work God has done there. Don Cormack's book *Killing Fields, Living Fields* details the tragedies, triumphs and miracles of this fascinating land. It is a book that should be read by anyone who has an interest in the Far East.

I wish to thank my editor, Irene Howat, who welcomed me so warmly into her home. I had many fears and apprehensions over the manuscript, but her gentle sensitivity and professional, skilful editing assured me that any doubts I had over publishing the book were unnecessary.

Finally, we are full of gratitude for the encouragement, love and care we have received from our pastors and the congregation of Goldhill Baptist Church. We are also indebted to Southeast Asian Outreach which unexpectedly provided us with our extended family.

CHAPTER ONE

AUGUST 11th 1956

DEATH'S DARK VALLEY

It was a warm sunny day, with white clouds blowing across the deep blue sky. I had every reason to feel happy and excited as my fiancé collected me from my home in Guildford and we drove to Swanage for a day's sailing. Lionel's family had a lovely coastguard cottage as a holiday home, and his parents and sister were spending the summer by the sea. When we arrived at the cottage quite a strong wind blew up. Postponing our sail, we decided to walk along the Downs at Peveril Point. As we stood watching the sea birds on the rocky coastline Lionel said, 'The wind's moderated, let's go back to the house and get ready for a sail.'

Lionel's father was out looking for us when we reached the cottage. 'Brenda, come quickly. There's a phone call for you.' I took the phone and heard my father's anxious voice. 'Come home as soon as possible. Philip's been involved in a terrible road accident at Northampton. He's in hospital and we must go as soon as you get home.' I assured him that we would leave immediately, but as I tried to tell Lionel what had happened, the walls began to spin round and I fainted. Within a short time, however, we were back in the car and speeding towards Guildford. The journey seemed endless, but as I thought of my lovely family I felt sure everything would be all right.

Most people would think my background rather odd and some might consider it deprived. My parents were Exclusive Brethren – a very strict sect of Christians who lived extremely disciplined lives. We had no radio or television, not even a record player. Smoking, dancing and the cinema were all banned, as were fashionable clothes, make-up, nice hairstyles and jewellery. We were not allowed friendships outside the Fellowship and marriage to an outsider was forbidden. Despite these strict rules and regulations we were a close and happy family.

I had three brothers, one a year older than me, Philip, three years younger, and the youngest followed nine years after Philip. My father was a bank manager but he had to retire prematurely after a year in hospital. Two years later he was able to resume work and was financial adviser to Cow and Gate. The illness left him with heart trouble but he spent all his spare time with the Brethren. He was a gifted preacher and teacher. In the home I respected his strict discipline because he was a very good father. He told us interesting stories and could play any tune on the piano by ear. Philip played the harp and my mother had a lovely singing voice. My older brother inherited Mother's talent and we sometimes spent free evenings enjoying music together as a family. I had lessons on both piano and violin. We were not, however, allowed to attend public concerts. Other Exclusive Brethren families did not encourage classical music, regarding it as 'worldly'. Both my brothers found the restrictions irksome. I hated the rules over dress and fashion as I did not see that anything was gained by looking dowdy. My 'worldly' dress and hairstyle caused several raised eyebrows amongst my fellows.

Philip was doing his National Service in the Army at Chester and it was rumoured amongst the Brethren that he had made friends in the Army and had been seen smoking. He was a very handsome and generous young man who was loved by the girls. One evening he was seen going into a cinema. This caused consternation amongst Brethren all over the country and eventually my brother was excommunicated. Philip was deeply upset and Father, who felt the judgement was too harsh, was shocked by what happened. It was a disgrace if one's family did not conform to the Brethren's teachings in such matters.

After leaving school in 1951 I trained as a Medical Laboratory Technician and worked as a food analyst for two years with Cow & Gate, a company then owned by Exclusive Brethren. Needing further experience I left and did two years research in Bovine Tuberculosis at the Veterinary Research Laboratories at Weybridge, then took a post as Research Assistant to Professor Stacey in the Department of Therapeutics and Pharmacology at St. Thomas's Hospital, London. I worked long hours on a research programme into stomach and bowel cancer. During that time I formed a close friendship with one of the doctors who worked in the laboratory, but, when I realised the implications of this association, I broke it off. I would have been in danger of being excommunicated by the Brethren and ostracized by my family had it continued. It was very hard at the time. Later Lionel began to visit our home. He was my older brother's closest friend. We fell in love and were engaged to be married. Because Lionel was a member of the Brethren our relationship met with no opposition.

Lionel drove at high speed from Swanage, and it was a relief when we finally reached my home in Guildford. I ran in to find the doctor attending to my father, who had suffered a mild heart attack after hearing about Philip's accident. The doctor told me to stay with Father until the emergency was over. Mother had already left for the hospital. The hours dragged past as we waited for the telephone to ring. Finally, late at night, she phoned and begged me to break the news to Father gently. Philip was critically ill. Both legs had multiple fractures, he had serious head injuries and his right arm had been amputated. My brother was just nineteen years old. I told Father the news and then sat with him for some time before going to my room. As I knelt by my bed that night and poured out all my distress to my loving heavenly Father, I asked him to help me face tomorrow and give me the strength I needed. Although I could not bear the thought of my younger brother going through life disfigured and with no right arm, I felt the calm of the presence of the Lord. Despite the awful events of the day I slept well.

Sunday morning dawned warm and sunny. Suddenly I remembered it was my mother's birthday and thought of her. She was very beautiful with dark fine hair, a flawless complexion and huge blue eyes. Thanks to her our home was always welcoming, with flowers artistically arranged and beautifully cooked meals. Every Sunday we had visitors for lunch and tea. These were usually visiting preachers and their families, students from the local college and anyone who needed help or comfort. This Sunday was very different. After breakfast the doctor called to see my father. Although he seemed to be a little better the doctor advised

17

me to stay at home with him. We were both relieved when Mother phoned in the afternoon to say that she was being very well cared for by a Brethren nurse at the hospital who had arranged a comfortable bed for my mother in her own home. Philip had still not regained consciousness. Mother promised to phone us again later.

Exclusive Brethren are usually very warm and caring within their own circle. Most of them are hospitable, and at times of family difficulty they generally surround one another with care. News circulated quickly through the network of Meetings and that day I had phone calls from all over the country assuring us of prayer and support. My mother was a woman of great faith. In 2 Kings 4:26 (AV), the Shunammite woman was asked, 'Is it well with the child?' In the presence of death she answered, 'It is well.' Late that afternoon my mother phoned and in a barely audible voice she said, 'It is well. It is well. Philip has been taken home to be with the Lord.'

My memories of Philip's funeral are of the large number of people who came long distances, some even returning from holiday to be with us. The beautiful words of the opening hymn by P P Bliss, have remained with me to this day:

When peace like a river attendeth my way,
   when sorrows like sea billows roll,

whatever my lot thou hast taught me to say,
'It is well, it is well with my soul.'

In the ensuing months I examined my faith
deeply. Although I was converted when I was
thirteen, in many respects I realised that I had
accepted my parents' faith. It was during these
dark days, as I read my Bible afresh, that Christ
became very real to me and I experienced his
presence with me in a new way.

Lionel and I decided to get married in the
Spring, but before that another deep grief was to
hit my family. One cold February morning as I
sat down to breakfast, my mother was pleased
to see in the post a letter from my eldest brother.
He had been a tower of strength to us in our
sadness. As she read the letter she began to
tremble and grew very pale. Mother handed the
letter to Father and he read it. Finally they shared
the news with me. They were both in tears as
they told me that, through his work, my brother
had met a girl who was not a member of the
Brethren and that he intended to marry her!

Despite many lengthy meetings with the
Brethren to discuss the situation and Father's
attempts to persuade the couple to wait a while
before taking such a step, my brother was finally
excommunicated and we were told to have
nothing more to do with him. This harsh
judgement chilled me, especially as the

excommunication took place just before our wedding. But if I had not submitted to their judgement there would have been repercussions for me to face. With my own marriage so near, I did not want to jeopardize my standing with the Brethren, but in my heart I had no intention of cutting my brother off.

Our wedding, on March 23rd 1957, was a very quiet affair and, to my dismay, my eldest brother was not permitted to attend. In those days the Exclusive Brethren did not allow brides to wear white dresses. This was thought to be copying a tradition from the main churches and was therefore considered worldly. I wore a pretty turquoise brocade dress. The wedding was held in a Registry Office because Meetings were not licensed for marriages. As Lionel's family were Exclusive Brethren they all came to the wedding meeting. The Brethren personally showed us great love and kindness. Such love and such harshness make strange companions, but this was all part of life within the Exclusive Brethren.

When we came home from our honeymoon feeling rested and happy, I was concerned at the change in my mother. She had suffered a deep loss in the death of one son and the excommunication of another. Father told me he was arranging to take her to Switzerland for a holiday as she was exhausted and shocked by recent events. Just one month later she was admitted to hospital. When the doctors finally diagnosed terminal cancer, we were all stunned. I went to see my old employer at St. Thomas's Hospital, as we had worked on research into stomach and bowel cancers. My father said that he would spend any amount of money to get the best treatment for Mother, but Professor Stacey confirmed that there was very little hope. I found this hard to accept, feeling very strongly that these circumstances were there only as a test of our faith. God was so real to me and, as I firmly believed that he would completely heal my mother, I prayed morning and night for his intervention.

I returned home to nurse Mother when doctors at the hospital said that they could do no more for her. After a few weeks, when I was finding night and day nursing exhausting, a very dear woman in the Guildford Meeting arrived at our house. 'Off you go to bed,' she said to me. 'I've come to do the night nursing until I'm no longer needed.' How wonderfully God provided for all our needs at just the right time. As well as being a capable nurse, our friend was a delightful character with a lively sense of humour.

It was exactly a year after Philip's death, on my mother's next birthday, that she lapsed into a coma. Three days later, on my birthday, all hopes of her being healed were dashed. As I bent to kiss her goodnight she opened her eyes for a moment and just said my name, 'Brenda.' Filled with a terrible sense of fear I went to my room and knelt by my bed. With bitter tears I cried to God, begging him not to take Mother away on my birthday. Never in my life had I experienced such dark despair. But, as I knelt, a bright light shone in my room and a gentle voice said, 'It is I, be not afraid.' I stayed there, strangely calmed by God's presence and feeling the touch of his hand. As I got into bed I promised him, 'I will go with you anywhere as long as you stay with me.' I slept well and in the morning our nurse put her arm lovingly around my shoulders and led me into my mother's room. She had been taken home in the night.

My youngest brother was eleven years old. His whole world had fallen apart. In one year he had seen the complete break-up of our once happy family. Now only he and Father remained at home. We engaged a succession of house-keepers to care for them, but five over the course of the next two years brought a fair measure of instability into his life. On several occasions he ran away, eventually arriving at our home asking to be allowed to live with us.

After supervising the needs of my father's home, I tried to settle down to married life in Slough. Exclusive Brethren wives were not allowed to work and I soon had so much time on my hands that I became depressed. And I missed the good companionship I had enjoyed at Guildford, finding the Slough Meeting small and uninteresting in comparison. I explained to Lionel that I wanted to go back to work. Although he agreed to this, we decided it would be unwise to tell the Brethren. I soon obtained a job with a well-known pharmaceutical company. Three months later one of the Slough Brethren discovered that I was working and we had a visit from an elder. This angered me but, when threatened with being put out of the Fellowship, I was forced to 'repent'. My repentance, however, was outward only. As I read my Bible day by day, I began to question some of these extreme teachings.

At this time Jim Taylor, a new Exclusive Brethren leader from America, visited England and began teaching fresh edicts and rules. Gradually the warm and loving Fellowships became gatherings of people who feared what would happen next! If wives did not conform to the rules their husbands were encouraged to obtain divorces. Until then divorce was unheard of within the Movement. Eating meals with relatives in traditional churches was banned. Membership of any association was ruled as an unequal yoke (2 Corinthians 6:14). Large numbers left the Fellowship, causing much heartache and division within families. Thousands were affected in different ways. We had, for example, many eminent doctors in the Fellowship, and membership of the Royal College of Physicians and the British Medical Association was banned, as were professional bodies of solicitors and accountants. The spiritual value of our Bible studies decreased as frequent arguments arose over controversial matters. Eventually, all these rules were made law by Taylor, and many were excommunicated for not complying with this 'New Ministry'.

The Exclusive Brethren was a worldwide movement and each day we heard news from other places of divisions, quarrels and broken families. A reign of fear began in which people were afraid to say what they really thought about anything. Holidays were considered worldly and not to be tolerated, as were many other harmless pastimes and hobbies. Pet dogs and cats had to be put down as these were viewed as idols. The harshness of this new era seemed to have no limits.

I felt utterly despondent in a Fellowship that was no longer my home and my anchor. Lionel was working as a partner in his family business and we were expecting our first child. To have left the Fellowship at that point would have cost him his job and our mortgage. We were not allowed to have Building Society mortgages and the wealthy Brethren arranged loans at low interest rates, in effect mortgaging your home.

When I telephoned my father to tell him our first child was expected, he also had news for me. He had just become engaged. I was pleased for him and relieved not to have the responsibility of caring for his home. However, I felt very sad that someone else was taking my mother's place. It seemed that her memory was being forgotten. I still missed her dreadfully.

When our first child, Rosemary, was born, I was thrilled to have a daughter. Her second name, Vera, was after my mother. Three years later we had another daughter, Alison Dawn, and my days were fully occupied. I was determined to be a loving wife and a good mother. During this period the Brethren Meetings were full of discord, strife, envy and place-seeking as the new leadership resorted to expelling the older godly men and replacing them with young inexperienced Brethren. Women were, of course, never allowed to take part or to express their opinions.

Father, who was now remarried, kept in close contact with us. Although he was upset over the divisions, he was sure something would happen and the situation would be put right. Then trouble erupted in the Guildford Meeting when the younger men tried to take control. Father did all he could to keep both sides together, but one night he had no option but to walk out. When all the Brethren rallied round my father, Jim Taylor stepped into the situation. He gave orders for Father to be excommunicated. I was so angry when I heard the circumstances that I too decided to leave. I was given an ultimatum: either I accept the judgement on my father or I be put out of the Fellowship and have my husband divorce me with him having custody of the children. My two girls were the mainstay of my life. Faced with the possibility of losing them I reluctantly agreed to the judgement. It was then that I began to hate the Movement.

My stepmother and youngest brother remained in the Fellowship while my father was outside. I watched him at a distance as he suffered such humiliation and defeat. After three years of this treatment he gave in, submitted to the Brethren's views and was reinstated. But he lost his zeal and never preached again.

Many times I begged my husband to leave the Exclusive Brethren, but he was extremely worried about losing his job and having our mortgage called in. The girls were at private school and we could not have afforded their fees if that had happened. Sending them to private school seemed the only way of shielding them from some of the harsh rules. The children of Brethren were not even allowed to eat their lunch with other pupils at school. They were also banned from religious instruction, school assemblies and parties. Increasingly we led a double life, allowing the girls to participate normally at school but advising them not to let the Brethren know what they were doing. The strain of living in this way took its toll on my health. I could not sleep due to all the worry and conflict in my life.

We moved to a new house that we had designed ourselves. It was beautiful and I took great pleasure in choosing the furnishings and making attractive curtains and cushions. In our lounge we had both a piano and an organ and I tried to comfort myself with music. Drained and exhausted I found myself losing patience with Lionel and the girls. I felt a failure. I was not the perfect wife and mother I had hoped to be. Eventually I became ill and my doctor sent me to a specialist who admitted me to hospital. The girls went to stay with friends we had made in the Edinburgh Meeting. I was relieved to know that they were well cared for.

After several weeks in hospital having extensive tests the specialist told me he had found nothing wrong and advised that I went on holiday! Although holidays were banned we were allowed to stay with Brethren elsewhere. So we arranged to go to the South of France. The Meeting in Toulon was very different from what we were used to. As the French Brethren did not pay much attention to the new rules we even had Sunday tea on the beach while the girls swam in the warm waters with the children of the lovely French family with whom we stayed. With fine French cooking, hot sunshine and a relaxation of the rules, I began to feel much better.

Our holiday happiness, however, was brought to a sudden halt by a phone call from one of the elders in Slough. It transpired that while the American leader was taking meetings in Scotland his conduct caused a scandal which was reported in the national newspapers. Many of the Scottish Brethren left the Fellowship, setting up rival meetings. We were ordered to leave Toulon at once to attend a special meeting that had been organised for us at six o'clock the following morning in High Wycombe! There we were to state publicly whether we were backing the American leadership or not. Packing our bags hastily, we set out on the long drive to Le Havre. It was as we drove that we decided the time had come for us to leave the Brethren Movement. It was August 1970, and all our formative years had been spent in this repressive regime. Leaving it behind was a great relief, but we did not realise how difficult it would be to establish a new lifestyle in a normal church.

CHAPTER TWO

LIFE IN FREEDOM

There was a worldwide division over the leadership of the Exclusive Brethren, although many meetings remained undivided and merely left the main Fellowship. Lionel and I were the only ones to leave our local Meeting and we decided to give our resignations officially before contacting our families. I telephoned Father and told him what I had done, begging him to keep in touch as I still intended to lead a Christian life although attending some other place of worship. We had a long talk and he urged me to remain. His experience of being excommunicated had left him with a dread of ever being in that position again. Finally, Father said goodbye sadly and told me he could have no further communication with me.

The relief of being freed at last from the Fellowship I had grown to hate, though I loved many of the people in it, was marred by the knowledge that I now had no relative left in whom I could confide. My youngest brother was married and both he and his wife remained in the Brethren. As Lionel's family all left we had no problems with his job and the girls were able to stay at their school. We began attending an evangelical church in Slough and I found myself searching the Bible on issues I had not considered before. For instance, I had never heard women pray in a prayer meeting. At first I was shocked by it! There were so many small and large adjustments to make. And I felt extremely lonely because I had lost all my friends as well as my family.

The pastor was a deeply spiritual man who genuinely cared for us as a family. Rosemary and Alison were bewildered by our decision to leave the Exclusive Brethren and suffered because of it when they lost their many good friends within the Fellowship. It was a new life for them and many tensions and problems arose. We had been warned by the local elders that, when we left the Fellowship, God would send judgement on us and we could lose both our daughters, either to worldly influences or a road accident. Although I did not believe this threat, it did have an adverse effect on me. If the girls were ever late home that warning rang in my ears and it made me an overprotective mother. I had not learned to trust completely in the guidance and care of my heavenly Father.

Lionel had great difficulty in accepting an entirely new church, especially because he felt very strongly about women participating in church meetings. However, as he had always loved sailing and latterly even this was banned in the Exclusive Brethren, his first resolve was to make the most of his new freedom and buy a dinghy. The American leader who had caused such division was nicknamed Big Jim. Imagine our amusement when the first boat we bought was called *Mighty Jim*!

The youth fellowship in our church was very strong and both girls gradually made new friends through it. Lionel and I still held some extreme views on church matters and the pastor was a great help to us when we raised concerns. He suggested appropriate Bible readings and then followed up with visits to discuss issues with us. His love and shepherd care was invaluable to us in our period of transition. Without it we could easily have drifted away from the church altogether and made shipwreck of the faith. Sadly we had friends who left the Brethren at the same time as us whose marriages have broken up and who never attend church.

Although we were free from the restrictive practices, that freedom brought many tensions. The rigidity of the Exclusive Brethren structure created a great sense of security. It was also a very close-knit community and our leisure time had been spent entertaining one another in our homes. This practice seemed to be missing in other churches. We invited our new Christian friends to our home but they rarely returned our hospitality. I believe our strange background made us difficult people to get on with, as we were very intolerant of other points of view.

Our loving and caring pastor died suddenly of a heart attack. We were extremely upset. He had been a father figure at a time when I still had to come to terms with the fact that I would never see my own father again. Sometimes, when I felt isolated and lonely, I wrote letters to Father seeking his company. There were no replies and the telephone was always put down when I called. When my mother and brother died I gradually accepted the finality of their deaths, painful as that was. But to have Father alive and living only twenty five miles away, and to be totally rejected by him, caused a very deep wound.

We kept in touch with other Exclusive Brethren who had left the Fellowship. But it was depressing to hear of the constant break-up of families, husbands or wives leaving, and children not conforming to the rules. In the empty isolation these people faced many even resorted to suicide.

One rule Jim Taylor brought in was that everyone was to drink alcohol. He was given to drink himself. In a Movement that had been partly teetotal many found that large quantities of spirits helped to calm their overwrought minds. Coping with a new lifestyle added to their anxiety and before long many had serious drink problems. I knew of one man who had been an excellent preacher and an exemplary family man, but after leaving the Exclusive Brethren he eventually dropped out of society altogether and joined the down-and-outs. Such examples provided the new leaders of the Brethren with just the kind of fodder they needed to feed the flock. Fear and intimidation kept a large number from leaving. I had phone calls from some still in the Fellowship telling me that they could not face the consequences of leaving and trying to find a new spiritual home.

Total dependence on any system of Christian persuasion is dangerous as it can lead to a lack a personal communion with God. There is no substitute for the daily discipline of Bible reading and prayer. The great men of the Old Testament had a close personal walk with God. Moses, for example, communed with him face to face, and through him God's chosen people were led from slavery in Egypt to the Promised Land. The failures of these men of God are also recorded for us to read. No-one is infallible and we need to develop discernment, testing all that we hear by the Word of God.

A new younger man took the place of our much-loved pastor. The church was independent but allied to the Assemblies of God. We were, therefore, used to hearing people speaking in tongues. I believe this is a gift of the Spirit, but it is not the greatest gift. Paul exhorts the Christians in Corinth to seek the gift of prophecy and concludes, 'Therefore, my brothers, be eager to prophesy, and do not forbid speaking in tongues. But everything should be done in a fitting and orderly way' (1 Corinthians 14:39-40).

The new pastor taught emphatically that Christians only have the Spirit if they speak in tongues. We could not agree with such extremism, having heard many gifted preachers in our mid-week Bible study who taught with authority that was clearly inspired by the Spirit yet who did not speak in tongues. New forms of worship were introduced that seemed to lack the reverence needed to worship a holy God. These and other issues that arose finally caused us to leave.

We found it very difficult to find a real spiritual home but began to realise that we should not expect to have good teaching every Sunday. In many ways we are responsible for feeding ourselves on the Bible and from the many good reliable books that are available. Such books had been banned in the Exclusive Brethren. How we enjoyed the freedom to read about the lives of missionaries and the experiences of other Christians.

During that time I was reading James' epistle in my quiet time. 'What good is it, my brothers, if a man claims to have faith but has no deeds?

Can such faith save him? Suppose a brother or sister is without clothes and daily food. If one of you says to him, "Go, I wish you well; keep warm and well fed," but does nothing about his physical needs, what good is it? In the same way, faith by itself, if it is not accompanied by action, is dead' (James 2:14-17). This reading was a great challenge to me as I had always lived very comfortably, caring only for the needs of those within the Christian faith. I knew that my own faith in Christ and his redeeming blood on the cross was very real, but it lacked this other dimension of Christian living that is a very essential part of the whole. Then we heard a sermon that was to change our lives completely. I believe that God was teaching us not to put our faith in any denomination but to totally trust his Word and his will for the future.

'Is not this the kind of fasting I have chosen: to loose the chains of injustice and untie the cords of the yoke, to set the oppressed free and to break every yoke? Is it not to share your food with the hungry and to provide the poor wanderer with shelter – when you see the naked, to clothe him ... if you spend yourselves on behalf of the hungry and satisfy the needs of the oppressed, then your light will rise in the darkness, and your night will become like noonday. The Lord will guide you always' (Isaiah 58:6-7, 11). Lionel and I looked at each other as we listened to these words

35

being read by a visiting preacher at our new church, both convinced that God was speaking directly to us. We discussed this passage many times at home, and over the next three months it was repeatedly brought to our attention. My husband and I were in total agreement that we needed to begin a new life in the Lord's service, but we needed further leading on what he wanted us to do. We made this matter a daily part of our prayer time, asking the Lord to show us in an unmistakable way what his way forward for us was.

Nearly forty years of our lives had been spent within the rigidity of the Exclusive Brethren's dogmatic teaching. Yet freedom from that strange oppression was not easy to handle. We had many struggles to overcome as we sought to keep the right balance in our day-to-day lives. There were far too many times when my mind went over the past and I thought of all I had lost, especially the love of my family. I had bouts of severe depression and often visited the graves of my mother and brother. On one of these occasions I decided to call and see Father. My hands shook as I parked the car outside my old home. I walked fearfully up the drive to the front door and rang the bell. When Father answered the door I was so pleased to see him that I flung my arms round him and burst into tears. He stood back slowly and looked at me with a cold, hard expression I had never seen before. 'Why have you come? You have no right to be here. Go home.' I stared unbelievingly at this hard, cold man who was once my affectionate father. He shut the door firmly.

'Your light will rise in the darkness, and your night will become like the noonday' (Isaiah 58:10). Having experienced much of the night and the darkness, I had many painful memories that increasingly weighed me down. I prayed that God would lead me to others who had lost their families, so that in caring for them I would forget myself.

A week later we were relaxing in the lounge of our home in our lovely Buckinghamshire village. It was autumn, and the surrounding countryside, the trees and woods where the deer grazed, was a blaze of colour. I loved this quiet location and was enjoying the challenge of our large garden. We switched on the television as there was a documentary on Cambodia, *Year Zero*, being shown. From 1970 to 1975 a civil war had raged throughout that country, which in peaceful times was known as 'the tourists' paradise of the Far East'. The devastation caused by the war was terrible. Millions of people were displaced by the fighting and the majority of the remaining population was sickened and exhausted by the continual violence. No-one envisaged that a four-year reign of terror by the infamous Pol Pot would follow these tragedies. He systematically destroyed the country's culture, religion and government, exterminating most of the intelligentsia and thousands of other victims on 'The Killing Fields'.

The programme showed hundreds of thousands of people who had been brutally uprooted from their homes and country, seeking the relative safety of the refugee camps on the Thai-Cambodia borders. Western aid agencies were trying to provide the basic necessities of life for these terrified people. We were both shocked and appalled by their suffering. By the end of the programme we had no doubt whatever that they were the poor we must help.

As we prayed for God to lead us in the right direction, we attended our usual monthly branch meeting of Gideons International. A letter was read stating that Head Office had English/ Vietnamese Bibles for distribution to any refugees who might be in our area. I volunteered to take responsibility for this, and the next day telephoned the local housing department to find out the addresses of any such refugees. The information was not available but I was given another number to ring. I put the call through saying that I was from Gideons International.

There was a pause and the man unexpectedly said, 'If you are from Gideons you must be a born again Christian.'

'Yes, that's correct,' I replied. 'But who am I speaking to?'

'This is Paul Penfold of Southeast Asian Outreach. We are a Christian mission originally called Cambodia for Christ and we've just finished a prayer meeting during which we asked the Lord for voluntary workers in the Slough area. Would you be interested?'

When I heard of their mission to help, house and care for the needs of Vietnamese and Cambodian refugees coming to this country, I knew at once that this was the leading we had waited for. I had a meeting with the Director of Southeast Asian Outreach the following week, and thus began an entirely new phase of life that was to be used of God to turn 'all the darkness into light'.

CHAPTER THREE

NEW FAMILY

It was a bright, crisp autumn morning in 1979. The sun shone through the trees as I walked happily towards the station to catch the train for London. The British Refugee Council had written to me, as they were working along with Southeast Asian Outreach on the resettlement of Vietnamese and Cambodian refugees. I was to attend a one day seminar to help me understand the many problems that these people face as they begin a new life in our country. Already I had visited three families who had been housed in Slough and was surprised at the very warm reception they gave me. In spite of the language problems we were able to communicate quite well. It was my responsibility to see that they attended English classes and then to help them find employment.

One of the families in my care was a widower with six children. His wife had died of tuberculosis while in a refugee camp. The youngest child, a little girl of four, had been successfully treated for TB but was now very neglected. The father, who was still depressed, was not coping well with his motherless children. Having experienced what my own home felt like without a mother, I spent a lot of time with this family. Gradually I was able to watch them adapt to our strange ways. When they became more confident with the language they accepted an invitation to our home for Sunday tea.

The father told us that he had heard about the Christian faith at a reception centre and now wanted to know more. They came to our church a few times, but it is extremely difficult for people to learn about the gospel in a language that is not their own. Through Southeast Asian Outreach I was told of a monthly service held at Bracknell by a former Chinese Missionary. All the refugees in our care who wished to attend were taken to these services. There, over tea, they had an opportunity to meet Vietnamese refugees from other areas.

In my spare time I read as many books as I could about Vietnam and Cambodia in order to learn about their culture. Southeast Asian Outreach asked me if I would like to take on the care of two refugees newly arrived from Saigon. They had spent several weeks in a reception centre where they had quickly learned some English and adapted well to our customs. The local council provided them with a small two bedroomed house not far from us and it was my responsibility to furnish it. I thoroughly enjoyed searching for good second hand furniture, making curtains and preparing their home for them.

From the British Refugee Council's paperwork we knew that Minh and Anh, who were coming to us, had escaped from Saigon when their eldest brother was arrested and imprisoned. The family had all been employed in the Navy under the American forces. When America pulled out of the Vietnam war, the South Vietnamese people who had helped America to defend their country against communism were rounded up and sent to prison or re-education camps. Minh's eldest brother, an influential man, had been a Commander in the Navy under the American forces. Just before he was captured, his wife and four children were taken to safety in America. As Minh had also served in the Navy he and Anh escaped before they too were arrested. In the Mid China Seas their boat began to sink and they were rescued by the SS *Ashford* and brought to England.

It was an exciting day when I first met Minh and Anh. I had put the finishing touches to their home and prepared a meal to welcome them. Lionel and I felt instantly drawn to them. Anh was twenty three years old, very small and pretty, while Minh was a few years older, quiet and shy. Little did I realise then that through this link I would later visit a Christian church in Vietnam.

After they had settled into their home both of them told me they did not want to attend daytime language studies as they wanted to work

42

immediately and study in the evenings. Anh explained that she had been a history student at Saigon University but the war had interrupted her studies. She decided to work in the electronics field. But, as she had had no experience at all, I pointed out that finding work might be difficult. Minh's job in the Navy had involved maintenance of air conditioning and refrigeration. His grasp of English was only fair. I explained to them that I was a Christian and believed in a living God who heard and answered prayer and that we would be praying for them. Each day after my Bible reading I brought the needs of these refugees to the Lord, knowing how much greater his love for them was than mine. We had experienced the loving detail of God's care for them as we furnished their home. Our church friends gave willingly and helped us with practicalities such as carpet laying and curtain hanging.

The Monday morning after Minh and Anh arrived was spent telephoning electronics companies to ask if they had any vacancies and contacting refrigeration repair services with a view to finding a job for Minh. I had two positive replies and was asked to accompany them to interviews. Minh was offered a job repairing refrigerators at an extremely low rate of pay. He insisted on taking it, as he did not want to accept any more help from our government. Anh's interview was with a large international company. Although she managed the verbal interview with the personnel manager very well indeed, I had doubts about her success when she was asked by the work's manager to demonstrate her practical skills. After quite a long time the work's manager came back to talk with me. 'She's quite good,' he said. 'She must have had some experience in Vietnam. Do you know about her experience?' 'Well yes,' I replied quietly, 'she has had many experiences in Vietnam.' I dared not say any more! Finally Anh came back into the room and, with a big smile on her face, she hugged me and said, 'I've got the job!' As we drove back to their home I asked Anh how she had managed a soldering iron for the first time. She laughed and said that she had watched the other workers carefully while the personnel manager talked to her. She was just determined to do this work!

That same evening we had a prayer time together to thank the Lord for answering prayers. Anh and Minh started work the same week but I felt rather concerned when I heard how high Anh's wages were in comparison to Minh's. They went to evening classes and kept their little home beautifully. One month later I had a telephone call from the manager of Anh's company. He said they were so delighted with her that he wondered if I knew of any other refugees who would like to be considered for a similar job! I told him about Minh and his acceptance of the refrigeration job on the very low wage. 'You must bring him along as soon as possible,' he said. 'It speaks well for him that he's prepared to work for so little.' When I met Minh from work that day and told him the news he was very pleased, especially as he had just been told that his company could not keep him on because they had insufficient work. Minh was accepted by the electronics company and began work there the following Monday.

As both Minh and Anh saw God answering our prayers and supplying all their needs, they began to put their faith in him. It took time for them to understand the Christian faith as they had been brought up in a Buddhist family. But it was very rewarding to see Anh opening up to the gospel as a flower opens to the rising sun. She had such a sweet nature combined with great strength of character that it was easy to love her. Minh was quieter and more reserved. He found it difficult to believe in a God who answered prayer. Although he progressed in work and earned enough money to buy a car, he became quieter and depressed.

Anh bought herself a small motor bike and soon passed her test. There were very few spare evenings for her as she continued her English studies and embarked on an electronics course at the local college. I told her that I was concerned about Minh as he didn't seem to be happy. I wondered what was worrying him. She explained he was upset about Hai, his eldest brother. Hai, who was twenty years older than Minh, had been imprisoned by the communist authorities in Vietnam because, as a Commander in the Navy under the American forces, he had defended his country against communism. Minh was sad that he had freedom, a job and a car while his brother was still in prison. And he was sure his brother would never know freedom because high ranking officers were given long sentences, then sent to re-education camps. Hai had a wife and four children in America. They occasionally wrote to Minh but rarely mentioned their father. Minh suspected that Hai's wife would seek divorce and find someone else.

As the weather turned colder I discovered that the widower's family did not have adequate warm clothing, and neither did Minh and Anh. We all enjoyed a day shopping with the widower's children. And Anh's good English enabled her to interpret for me when any misunderstandings in the language arose. I had gladly spent quite a large sum of money from my monthly housekeeping allowance on their needs and, at the end of that very week, a cheque came in the post from a Christian friend who wished to share with us in our new ministry. It was for the exact amount we had spent on clothes, and it came before I had even told Lionel that I had used the housekeeping money! How lovingly our heavenly Father confirmed us in this new work. Every Sunday we had a large gathering at our home for lunch and tea. There was always plenty of laughter, usually over language mistakes. The refugees soon became our extended family and frequently came with us to the evening services at our church.

How cruel is war in any land! We have heard a great deal of the suffering of American servicemen, but little is known about people like Hai, victims of the war in Vietnam. I thought carefully about his situation and was led to read the Lord's words. 'He has sent me to proclaim freedom for the prisoners and recovery of sight for the blind, to release the oppressed' (Luke 4:18). In simple faith I took this scripture to the Lord in my prayer time and asked that Hai be released from prison. Two other Christian friends shared my concern and we started a weekly prayer meeting at our home to bring the needs of our refugee family to the Lord. I went to see Minh and told him that I believed God could open prison doors and set prisoners free. The depth of his love and concern for Hai showed as he quickly wiped away tears.

Minh soon had a friend, as another Vietnamese young man was placed in my care. Tien, who had lived near Hanoi in North Vietnam, was half way through a university course when the war interrupted his studies. He hated communism and all the damage it did to his country. The communist officials harassed people of Tien's social standing and university education. Tien had an older brother whom he had brought with him to support. The brother, who was in his forties, had been interrogated and beaten on so many occasions that he suffered a severe mental breakdown. He was very disturbed and sometimes lost control of himself. On other occasions he went missing, which was a particular concern as he knew no English. He was diligently cared for by his young brother. Tien quickly mastered the language and looked for work in order to pay for further education. He obtained employment with an engineering company and joined Minh and Anh for English studies in the evenings. As we found Tien a very sensitive, caring young man, we were delighted when he asked if he could come along to our church services.

Most of these young people had lost one or both parents and several other relatives in the war. They came here with a background of war, food shortages, fear and broken families in the refugee camps. I found it easy to relate to them and looked back on my own experiences with a new light. I needed those dark years of discipline in the school of God to help equip me with the compassion that was essential to care for these broken people.

Southeast Asian Outreach, which had opened a centre in Gravesend for Cambodian refugees who had been given political asylum in this country, telephoned me one day to say that they needed help with accommodation. As part of my husband's business was a property trust, I told him of the need and asked if he had any vacant properties to let. Lionel was a great support to me in this work, but he laughed at my question about vacant properties. 'We rarely have a vacancy,' he explained. 'Our rents are so low that tenants rarely leave. I'm afraid we can't help.' 'If that's the case,' I replied, 'I am going to pray that a flat will become vacant for the Cambodian refugees. That's our primary calling.' He smiled at my enthusiasm.

A week later he came home tired and irritated. 'I've an exceptionally busy week and, to add to my problems, tenants have left one of the London Road flats in the middle of an agreement and without paying any bills.'

'An answer to prayer!' I replied smiling.

'Well I didn't look at it like that. What are you saying?' he asked.

'Can we offer the flat to the Southeast Asian Outreach to house some Cambodian refugees?'

Lionel agreed. So I was able to telephone that

afternoon to say that we had one property available to house two refugees. I was told they had two sisters who had recently come from a Thai refugee camp and who needed a lot of support. They had been through the Killing Fields, eventually escaping from Cambodia by walking through forests at night to a refugee camp on the Thai-Cambodian borders. A week later, with the flat freshly cleaned and polished, flowers on the table and a meal prepared, we welcomed Thida and Boppha.

What sweet girls the sisters were, with their shining black hair and dark eyes that easily clouded with fear and apprehension. After the meal I showed them round the flat, waited while they put away their few belongings, then introduced them to the local shops. The next few days were spent enrolling them at college and teaching them a little of our English way of life. They were so eager to learn. Soon they were able to tell me that they were both in their early twenties and that they wished to learn dressmaking. Neither of them spoke sufficient English to go to dressmaking classes but we managed to hold a reasonable conversation on the subject with the assistance of sign language!

Having lent them my electric sewing machine, they asked if they could make me a dress. I decided to take them to London for a day, thinking that would allow them to see the city and visit a departmental store to choose material. Those early days with Thida and Boppha were an exciting adventure for all of us. I shall never forget the expression on their faces when we stood looking at the huge variety of fabrics in a West End store! Thida looked at me in astonishment and said, 'This shop is very big. It must be a government shop.' 'No,' I replied. 'We don't have government shops in England. All the shops you have seen are privately owned.' 'Oh, that's amazing!' she replied softly, eyes wide with astonishment. It was a delightful task showing Thida and Boppha how we lived. They responded so quickly. Only six months later the language tutor at the college phoned me to say that Thida was at the top of the English class, having beaten all the European students in the year!

The dress they made me was so beautifully sewn that we decided to lend them the capital for two electric sewing machines and set them up as private dressmakers. Thida insisted that they take classes in English style tailoring and dressmaking but, before the end of the year, I had a phone call from the class teacher. She could not understand why I had enrolled the girls as the standard of their work was so high that she said they could have taught the class!

Christmas 1980 was very special as we invited our five foster children to share our Christmas

CHAPTER FOUR

UNEXPECTED ARRIVALS

Life was busy and rewarding as I continued to look after the needs of our five foster children. In addition to them, I had the care of three other Vietnamese families who had been resettled in our area. There were many and varied problems. The widower with six children suffered from such severe depression that he gave up caring for his family. His eldest daughter frequently phoned me late at night upset that her father had gone out and she did not know when he was coming back. I would go to their house, settle the other children in bed, then wait up with her until their father came back. The situation became so difficult in 1980 that I involved Social Services and one of their staff was a great help in guiding this needy family. During the winter many of the refugees suffered severe bouts of bronchitis and influenza, so unaccustomed were they to our weather. As time went on I observed the younger ones adapting while the older refugees continued to have problems with the language and often felt depressed, homesick and lonely.

There was a support group formed in our local churches but after a year no-one continued with it, leaving me all the refugee problems to solve on my own with Lionel's support! I remembered back to our initial elation at being freed from the oppression of Exclusive Brethrenism, then the feeling of loneliness and alienation as we sought to adjust to our new lifestyle. How perfect was our heavenly Father's training for this work, and daily we proved his great faithfulness in supplying all our needs.

One lovely spring afternoon the following year I came home after visiting all the families and picked up my Bible to have my quiet time. The reading was in James' Epistle. I was strangely attracted to one verse. 'Religion that God our Father accepts as pure and faultless is this: to look after orphans and widows in their distress and to keep oneself from being polluted by the world' (James 1:27). I thought about the many aspects of practical Christian living and then of my extended family's needs. I remember very clearly kneeling in prayer, telling the Lord that this verse about the care of orphans had not attracted my attention in the same way before, but I was already looking after five young people although none of them were actual orphans. Having more than enough to do, I did not need orphans as well.

The telephone interrupted my prayer time. 'This is the Welfare Office of Heathrow Airport,' a voice said. 'We have been in touch with Slough

Social Services who gave us your number as apparently you look after some refugees.'

'That's correct,' I replied. 'I work on a voluntary basis for the British Refugee Council and Southeast Asian Outreach on the resettlement of Vietnamese and Cambodian refugees.'

'Well,' the caller went on, 'we have two orphan boys here in our office who arrived at Heathrow today from Burma and because of their ages we do not know where to place them. They are not eligible to go into an orphanage and they appear such nice young lads that we hesitate to put them in a hostel. Would you be prepared to care for them for a few days?'

'Did you say they were orphans?' I asked.

'Yes, orphans from Burma. It's a long journey from Burma to England and they're tired.'

I thought of that verse from the Epistle of James and felt this could only be God speaking to me. I agreed to take them and told the Heathrow authorities that I would leave immediately and travel by car to the airport.

When I walked into the Welfare Office at Heathrow I saw the boys sitting there in smart western clothes. They were nice looking lads, and I guessed their ages at about eighteen or nineteen years old. The lady in charge explained that they were brothers and assured me that should I have any queries I could contact her at any time. She handed me their passports and I observed that they were British citizens living in Burma who had been repatriated here. With the two small boxes that accompanied them, the boys and I got into my car and we drove back to Burnham.

The eldest boy, Stephen, spoke some broken English but the younger one, Christopher, could not speak a word. I explained that we lived in a village outside London and that I had two grownup daughters and five foster children, three of them from Vietnam and two from Cambodia. Stephen translated what I said for his brother. When we arrived home I showed them to a spare bedroom and suggested they took a rest before meeting my husband for dinner at 6.30.

As my mind was occupied with the need to have enough dinner for our two unexpected guests, I drove to the local butcher and bought some extra meat. In my preoccupation with the meal, I completely forgot to telephone Lionel to tell him about the boys! He walked in at 6.30pm, briefcase in hand, just as the boys came down the stairs dressed in Burmese longyis! This Burmese traditional dress looks like a long skirt.

'What on earth have we got here?' Lionel asked in amazement. 'Are they Moslem priests or something of the sort? Haven't you got enough to do with the five others? Wherever did you get them from?'

'Sshh!,' I replied quickly, 'The eldest one speaks a bit of English! I'm really very sorry I forgot to phone you. They're orphans from Burma. I'll explain it all to you in the study after dinner. Let's eat now.'

It is our custom to thank God for our meals. When Lionel had said grace Stephen looked up in surprise. 'Praise God!' he said, 'Is this a Christian home?'

'Yes, Stephen, it is. Are you a Christian?' I asked in surprise, as I knew Burma to be one of the most Buddhist countries in the world.

'Yes,' he replied. 'I'm a Christian.' Stephen smiled and then translated the conversation for Christopher. Christopher also looked very happy.

'How did you become a Christian?' I asked the older boy.

In broken English he replied, 'I was born in London, mother English and father Burmese student. My mother disappeared and my father put us in an orphanage in London and then flew back to Burma. My father drank too much. He told my uncle about us. My uncle is a big man in Immigration in Burma. He was shocked to know we were in England. He sent for us to come to Burma and we were brought up there by our Buddhist uncle and Moslem aunt. My father a Moslem. We live sixteen years in Burma and my father die. Burmese government said, "You British citizens and can't stay here now father dead. So we send you back to England." '

Stephen continued his explanation. 'I'm very sad and upset so I start to look for a real and living god to help me. I looked in Chinese temple and Roman Catholic Church but no living god there. Each day I ask, if there is a real god, please tell me. One day some boys near our home asked me to go to their church. I go and find living God with them. He is Jesus. You won't understand about these Christians because they are small group in the church. They are strict, don't smoke and drink. You won't have heard of them. They are called Brethren. When government officer tell me you go back to England, me and my friends we pray each day. Please God, send me to Christian house because I never live in one.'

We listened in amazement to his story as we continued with our meal. I explained to Stephen that we certainly did know about this group as both Lionel and I had been bought up in the Brethren. I hasten to add that there were no Exclusive Brethren in Burma, but there are several churches from the mainline Christian Brethren and they are as well known there for their devotion to Christian principles as they are here. Afterwards, as I talked with Lionel in the study about my Bible reading on the care of orphans, he too felt that this was clearly the hand of God.

Our main concern was what we were going to do with the boys as neither of them knew the language well enough to get a job. The papers they had from the British Embassy in Rangoon explained that they had been left in a London orphanage when they were two and three years old respectively. No-one had traced their mother's whereabouts and, as there was only her name and no dates of birth on their birth certificates, it was impossible to trace her. Their father had been sent to England by the Burmese government to take an engineering course on the understanding that he was not to get involved with English women and definitely not to marry. At that time Burma had gained independence from British rule and the government was very anti British. Although the boys' father knew he would be in trouble, he married and asked his wife to accompany him back to Burma. She refused and walked out of his life. He was extremely upset and started to drink heavily. On his return home he did not tell the authorities about his marriage or his sons. But his sister was concerned when he told her. As her husband held an important position in the Immigration Department, they sent a friend to England to collect the children from the orphanage and had them flown to Burma on British passports.

British citizens resident in Burma have to hold a Foreign Resident's Card (FRC) which is renewed annually for a hefty fee. But the boys' aunt and uncle decided that it was in their own interests not to disclose to the authorities Stephen and Christopher's nationality nor to tell the boys of their true parentage. Their father, whom they knew only as an uncle, lived nearby but was an alcoholic. Thirteen years later the boys' grandparents died within three months of each other. Their grandfather had been a high court judge in Rangoon. His estate was divided between his son and daughter. On inheriting the money the boys' father suddenly demanded to have his sons back and bought a house in which they could live with him.

When this happened the boys, who were sixteen and seventeen years old, were suddenly told the truth of their parentage. Christopher couldn't cope and started drinking heavily, whereas Stephen shook off his Buddhist / Moslem upbringing and began to search for a god to help him. The change of home was a huge upheaval for them, and coming to terms with the truth that their drunken uncle was in fact their father added greatly to their trauma. The boys had to live with his bouts of drunkenness and violent conduct. Stephen tried to get medical care for him but in Burma there is little help for alcoholics. Finally their father died after a heavy drinking session, actually cursing God in his last moments. This terrified the boys. When they registered their father's death with the authorities, their own nationality came to light from their birth certificates. They were asked to pay the heavy fee for the FRC card, but all their father's money had gone on drink and the house had to be sold to pay his debts. The boys were homeless and neither of them was prepared to return to their uncle and aunt.

For a while they both wandered about, sometimes spending the nights at friends' homes. As they could not pay for their FRC cards the Burmese authorities said they must be repatriated to England where they could probably find their mother. Christopher, who had a friend in the Baptist church, accepted the Christian faith and gave up drinking and smoking. Stephen was converted through the Christian Brethren. (I put the facts together some time later when I received letters from their uncle.) While it would have been understandable for the boys' uncle and aunt to be very sad that they had abandoned their Buddhist and Moslem upbringing, Stephen and Christopher's conversions had the effect of making them actually hate Christians, as I was to discover for myself a few years later when I visited Rangoon.

My Vietnamese and Cambodian young people continued to make good progress. Anh passed her first examination in electronics and was top of the class. Minh seemed to become more content as I assured him that Hai was continually in my prayers. However, I did explain that we have to wait for God's perfect time for the answers to our prayers. Tien's job was rather mundane but he told me that his goal was to become proficient in the language, save as much money as he could, and go to college to continue his studies. Such was his personality that I felt it possible that he would succeed. Tien had applied for his elderly mother, who was still in Vietnam, to come to the UK as a dependent relative. Passports and exit visas take several years to obtain in Vietnam, and are often almost unobtainable unless bribes are paid. His father had died in the war.

Stephen and Christopher were introduced to our five other foster children and they soon became good friends. Our Sundays were enriched by the Burmese boys' musical talents. After the evening service we all had supper together and then sang songs. I accompanied the boys' guitars on the piano. On such happy and relaxed occasions as these I did not envisage quite what a daunting task caring for these two orphan boys would become. Life was full of surprises with them and at times difficult. Stephen was extremely volatile and lost his temper over very small things. Although Christopher was more easy going he did not get on well with his brother. They had frequent fights which I had to stop before even trying to find out what had caused them.

It had its lighter moments too. When I went out shopping one day very soon after they came, I returned to find Stephen sitting on the roof of the house dressed in his Burmese longyi! Christopher was in the kitchen, busy cleaning the bell his brother had retrieved from the roof. They had discovered that our alarm system was not working and decided to repair it. The boys were skilled at repairing almost anything. Not wishing to spoil the new jeans I had bought them they had changed into their old longyis. Later that afternoon, and wearing the same attire, they cleaned my car in the drive. I had a phone call from a concerned neighbour. 'Brenda,' she said. 'There are two young fellows wearing skirts, and one minute they're shinning up and down your drainpipes and sitting on the roof, and the next they're cleaning your car! What's going on?' I laughed and explained about Stephen and Christopher. 'Well, I hope you know what you are doing,' she concluded.

I had a talk with the boys and asked them not to wear their longyis in the front of the house as people would wonder about it. They looked surprised and assured me that old longyis were the best of all clothes for doing odd jobs. I had to explain to them that they could be misunderstood in England if they were thought to be wearing skirts. People might get wrong ideas. They spoke in Burmese for a short time and then acted out a little scene looking like transvestites. 'That's right!' I laughed. 'So please don't wear longyis outside again!'

Lionel and I, having discussed the boys' future, decided to place them in a Christian language school where they could board during the week but come home for weekends. He found their high spirits rather too much to cope with after a tiring day at work. We were also very concerned at the effect the situation was having on our own girls. Rosemary was by then not living with us, but Alison was still at home. They had accepted the other five very well, but were understandably annoyed when, because of their background, we tried to be as lenient as possible with the boys. I certainly tolerated conduct from them that I would not have allowed with my daughters. Lionel and I both felt quite strongly that God had sent the boys to us and that we should continue to care for them until they were able to live independently.

One weekend a big dispute arose between Stephen and Christopher and, as they screamed at each other in Burmese, I didn't know what it was about. Finally the banging and crashing from their bedroom grew so loud that I ran upstairs and shouted, 'Stop all that at once and come down immediately!' They obeyed, but as neither of them was fluent in the language I did not succeed in discovering the problem. During dinner I noticed that Stephen ate very little. When I woke in the night and heard him walking up and down the stairs I went to investigate. He told me he had a big pain in his arm and neck and, fetching a dictionary, he added, 'My brother stabbed me.' I could see only a small puncture wound on his arm so, giving him a pain killer, I went back to bed.

The next evening we had friends for a dinner party. After introducing the boys we proceeded with the meal. Half way through the evening Stephen grew very pale and I noticed he was not eating. As there were several guests and it was a happy party, no-one else noticed Stephen's discomfort. He came into the kitchen when I was serving coffee and told me he had a terrible pain in his arm and neck. I excused myself from the company and drove him to the casualty department of our local hospital. The doctor who examined him found nothing wrong and advised me to give him codeine and make him rest for a few days.

That night Stephen had no sleep. Early in the morning I asked him to tell me what had happened. Requesting paper and pencil he drew a picture of a coconut tree and then an arrow to the centre of the trunk. 'I had comb for my hair made of this hard stuff. It's like metal. I can't find the handle any more. It's in my arm.' I immediately drove him back to the hospital and insisted that an x-ray be taken. Explaining that I had taken on the care of Stephen and his brother, I assured the staff that as they were British citizens they were entitled to health care. Then I added that there had been a fierce fight between the boys. The doctor looked at me with contempt and dismissed us. I went to the nearest telephone and called Lionel to ask if we could admit Stephen as a private patient, suggesting that we ask a Christian surgeon friend of ours to investigate the problem. He agreed, especially as it was coming very close to a holiday we had booked for seven of our extended family to come with us, cruising on the Norfolk broads. We needed a break and so did they.

I was really worried how Lionel would react if I told him the whole truth about the boys' violent fight. Thinking he might say that they must go, I did not disclose all the facts to him and passed it all off as a small accident. The Christian surgeon heard my story and acted speedily. Stephen was immediately x-rayed, and the x-ray showed a long object pressing on a nerve in the top of his arm. The surgeon said they must operate as soon as possible to save the use of his arm. Leaving Stephen in hospital I went home feeling tired and worried. We were due to go on holiday the following day.

Because the young people were all prepared and so excited about the holiday, I suggested to Lionel that he take them as planned, and that I remain at home and bring Stephen along as soon as he was better. When my husband left with the foster children I drove to the hospital to see Stephen, who was quite poorly. The surgeon passed me a jar with the foreign body in it. 'We are completely puzzled as to what this could be and how it could have lodged so deeply in his arm,' he said. I explained that there had been a very fierce fight and after it the long handle of a comb made from the centre part of a coconut tree was missing. The surgeon was most caring and understanding but advised me to tell Lionel exactly what had happened, assuring me that we were doing a wonderful job for the Lord in caring for these young people. I needed a word of encouragement at that moment as I must confess I was beginning to feel that I had taken on too much.

Three days later Stephen was discharged from hospital. We packed our bags hastily and I drove towards the Norfolk Broads, having spoken to my husband the previous evening and found that they were near Brundall. I prayed that God would lead me to the cruiser, as we had no means of communicating with Lionel. As I was driving slowly over a narrow bridge, I saw a large cruiser coming towards us with the young people on its

CHAPTER FIVE

EVERY NEED SUPPLIED

Life resumed a more normal pattern in the early summer of 1982 when both Stephen and Chris returned to board weekly at their Christian Language School. Chris made great strides with his English, but Stephen still struggled although he put in a lot of study time. I noticed that he did not look well and one weekend I found him asleep in his room at midday. On taking his temperature I discovered it was very high. Stephen's arm had healed and Chris, who was very upset at the seriousness of the injury, had asked for his forgiveness. Their relationship with each other did not improve when Stephen refused to forgive him.

I made an appointment for Stephen to see our family doctor. After a lengthy consultation he came into the room I was in. 'Can you get Stephen to the London Hospital for Tropical Diseases by midday?' he asked.

'Why, yes,' I replied. 'Is there something seriously wrong?'

'I don't know at this stage, but he certainly has a problem with his lungs and I want it checked as soon as possible. Take a seat while I telephone a doctor at the hospital.'

I looked at Stephen sitting pale and frightened and told him that we would take care of everything and he would be all right. The doctor confirmed the appointment and handed me a letter to give to the consultant.

Later that day, after Stephen had undergone many tests and x-rays, the consultant called me into his room. 'How long has Stephen been with you and your family?'

'Four months,' I replied.

He looked at the chest x-rays and said gravely, 'As you can see, both lungs are heavily infected. It looks like TB but I'm not one hundred percent sure at this stage. I'm concerned about you and your family as this is infectious.'

'It's not a problem with either me or my family,' I replied. 'I caught TB many years ago when I worked on a research programme on Bovine Tuberculosis at the Veterinary Laboratories, Weybridge. Aware of the infectiousness of this illness I asked that both my daughters be vaccinated against it when they were very young just in case it returned with me. I know this can happen sometimes. How ill is Stephen?' I asked, upset because despite all the problems I had begun to love these boys.

'He's very sick and must be admitted immediately. Have you brought his clothes?'

'No.' I replied. 'I didn't think his condition was so serious.'

I drove back to fetch Stephen's clothes and his paints. I thought painting would give him something to do.

A week later I was told that he did not have TB but Pulmonary Eosinophilia. This is a condition very much like TB when it affects the lungs. It is caused by a mosquito that exists in Burma. The consultant told me that had Stephen remained in Burma, he would almost certainly have died. I felt more convinced than ever that God's hand was over these boys and he was true to his promise that he will be 'a father to the fatherless' (Psalm 68:5).

After three weeks in hospital, the doctor asked me if it were at all possible for Stephen to go to a seaside resort as the clean air would help him. 'Why yes,' I replied. 'We have a caravan that's kept in a field at Swanage for the summer season. I could take him there.' The doctor said that was the best treatment for him and asked me to collect Stephen the next day, by which time he would have all the necessary medicines ready. I went to visit all my refugees and told them I would not be able to help for three weeks because of Stephen's illness. Chris was very concerned about his brother and the illness seemed to draw them closer together. The pair of us went to Swanage, but the holiday was not quite as easy as I had anticipated. Whatever I did for Stephen was wrong. He was very irritable and the temper

71

tantrums in the caravan were not amusing.

Towards the end of the first week I telephoned my husband. 'I can't sleep. I'm worried about Stephen and think that he may be better with someone else. I've really had enough of all the tempers and trouble!'

'Now calm down,' Lionel replied, 'I've been praying about this and we're definitely going to keep him. I'll come down with Chris at the weekend and we'll have a talk. Take a break yourself.'

'What!' I replied angrily. 'Take a break! What a joke! How can I take a break?'

Lionel answered, 'Why don't you go to the Women's Meeting at the Baptist Church? Leave the car outside and tell Stephen he can sit in it if it rains and if it's dry he can go for a walk. But he must be back by 9.30.'

'The Women's Meeting at the Baptist Church?' I repeated, still feeling annoyed. 'I've never been there before. I don't know anyone and anyway these meetings are for the over 60s – not my scene.'

'Now you go, dear, and I will be down on Friday night and sort things out,' Lionel replied firmly.

'Oh all right then, I'll go. But I can't see how it will help.'

At 7.30 that evening I sat down in a small room at the back of the Baptist Church and looked around. Sure enough, it was the over 70s club rather than the over 60s! I really felt quite out of place and was worrying about Stephen. Would he be in the car at 9.30? My mind wandered, probably because I'd had no sleep that week, having walked round the fields in the moonlight asking God to give me a deep love for the brothers. This was essential if we were to carry on, and I knew it. And I'd had no time for Bible reading either, and very little time for prayer. Stephen was so demanding.

To my surprise the pastor walked in and introduced the Bible study like this. 'I was praying over this little meeting this afternoon and felt that we should not continue our study of Luke's Gospel tonight. Instead we will read James chapter one. It would be nice if we read round taking two verses each.' Reading round! How I hated that method of reading. We had sometimes practised it in my home all those years ago. It distracted me and I could never get the gist of the reading. So I switched off and began to wonder what Stephen was doing. I thought of the weekend and began mentally planning the meals. Suddenly my arm was jogged by an elderly woman. 'It's your turn,' she whispered, 'verse 26.' So I read, 'If anyone considers himself religious and yet does not keep a tight rein on his tongue, he deceives himself and his religion is worthless. Religion that God our Father accepts as pure and faultless is this: to look after orphans and widows in their distress and to keep oneself from being polluted by the world' (James 1:26-27). 'Pull yourself together,' I said to myself, 'and pay attention now.'

The pastor explained he had been arrested by the last verse because if he had asked his congregation what the definition of a Christian was, he doubted whether anyone would have answered that it was to care for widows and orphans. He added that he had even wondered about the relevance of this teaching as he looked around his faithful sisterhood, most of whom were widows themselves and did not have the strength to care for orphans.

After the meeting the pastor came up to me and said, 'Are you on holiday here?'

'Well, I suppose you could call it a holiday,' I replied.

'Have you any problems you would like to share?' he asked kindly.

I told him about Stephen and the difficult time I was having, and that the Bible study had helped me. I mentioned that we were supposed to stay three weeks.

'Come to our service on Sunday and bring Stephen. It will do him good,' he said.

'Well, that's kind of you but he's going through a difficult stage. My husband's coming down at the weekend with Stephen's brother, but

I doubt if either of the boys will come as they are both refusing to go to services.'

'I'll pray for them,' the pastor assured me. Then he went on, 'It occurs to me that we have an elder here who may be able to help you through the rest of your stay.'

Thanking him for his kindness I left to see if Stephen was waiting. He was. I told him about the good Bible study and asked if he would like to go to the service on Sunday. He said he had no intention of going to church as he had no friends there and it was boring. However, he was far more amenable and that night I slept well.

Lionel arrived the next evening with Chris. The boys, who seemed very pleased to see each other, were fascinated with our holiday home on wheels as they had never seen anything like it in Burma. 'Hot water on tap and a flush loo!' Chris exclaimed. 'How does it all work?' When Sunday morning arrived they both agreed to attend the service. The church was packed, with a large number of holidaymakers swelling the numbers. After the service the pastor came over to speak to us and introduced himself to the boys, giving them a very warm welcome. How important it is to welcome strangers and foreigners who come to our churches. Sadly this is not always done and visitors can leave a service feeling unloved. I know how much it meant to our refugee family when people went out of their way to make them feel welcome, and how hard it was for them when that didn't happen.

The pastor that Sunday was so kind to us. He really cheered me and gave me the encouragement I needed. 'Wait a minute!' he said as we were leaving. 'I want to introduce you to one of our elders.' A tall, distinguished looking gentleman with grey hair came towards us and, as he looked carefully at me, his face lit up. 'You must be Brenda!' he said. 'I used to preach at your Brethren Meeting when you were a girl. Your father and I were friends.'

'I remember you!' I exclaimed. 'You're Dr. Smart! Fancy you remembering me after all these years!'

'You haven't changed much!' he laughed, shaking hands with Lionel and the boys. 'Come back to lunch with us and let me introduce you to my wife. She'll be delighted to meet you again.'

We went to his home for lunch and had a very happy time there. In God's plan this Christian doctor who was placed there to help us, was not just an old friend, he was also the retired Dean of Brompton Chest Hospital, London. With his expertise he knew all about Stephen's rare condition and was able to tell me that the drugs he was on would add to his personality problems. They were known to make patients irritable. Dr. Smart took Stephen and Chris for a long walk in the afternoon, then we all had tea together. He and his wife told me to call and see them during our stay and they promised to pray for both the boys and me. In the perfect ways of our heavenly Father I was given encouragement to continue, and all the support that I needed, both medically and spiritually.

The final weekend at Swanage was one to remember. Lionel came down to help me clear up and brought the Cambodian girls and Minh and Anh with him. We introduced the young people to the putting green and completed the course with some playful competition. As the last day was warm and sunny we all enjoyed a barbecue lunch in the farmer's field. Skylarks sang in the blue skies overhead and cows grazed contentedly in the field. The old coastguard cottage had been sold several years before but we went for a walk along the cliffs at Peveril Point before driving home. Twenty-four years had passed since my first visit to Swanage. How many changes there had been in that time! We had two beautiful daughters, and our lives and theirs had undergone great changes because of the work we had taken on. It was not always easy for either us or the girls but, through the many difficulties, we proved God's care. It is in the hard times of life that his presence is so real.

About six months later, in 1982, when Stephen had fully recovered from his illness and his grasp of English was good, he told me he did not want to stay at the language school but wished to start work. He had taken a course in Burma on radio assembly and repairs and wanted to work in something similar here. But the boy had one ambition greater than that, he wanted to trace his mother. Chris stayed on at the language school. When I asked him about tracing his mother he thought it would be nice but told me he felt I was his mother and he was quite content with things as they stood. Their mother's name was on their birth certificate but no other information was given. I spent several weeks trying to trace her both at Somerset House and through the Salvation Army Missing Persons Bureau, but without success. In reply to a letter I sent the boys' uncle in Rangoon, I was advised to stop any further attempts to trace her. He explained that he had met her in London several years before, that she had his address but had never contacted him. He was unimpressed at her complete lack of interest in the boys.

We were so pleased at the progress Chris made at language school both in English and, more importantly, as a Christian. One of the tutors observed his spiritual growth and when they had a special outreach meeting at the school she asked if he would be prepared to give his testimony. He told me all about it very enthusiastically. I attended the meeting and was thrilled to hear Chris very nervously tell everyone what the Lord had done for him in his life. He spoke sweetly of the power of Jesus he had experienced in overcoming drinking, smoking and occasionally taking drugs. As we enjoyed some refreshments together after the meeting I felt a very deep bond had been formed between us.

Stephen, who still lived with us, settled down well working for an electronics company. He received regular letters from Rangoon with a verse, 'The Lord watch between me and thee when we are absent one from another' (Genesis 31:49, AV), always written on the envelopes. When I asked him who the writer was, he showed me a photo of a pretty Burmese girl named Ponnie. She was a strong Christian who attended the Baptist Church in Rangoon. Her father, a Buddhist, did not like Stephen, but the girl's mother who was a deaconess in the Baptist church was kind to him. Stephen's girl friend was studying for a Bachelor of Science degree at Rangoon University.

Minh and Anh both got on well at work and Anh began to ask a lot of questions about our faith. I had given all the refugees a Gideon Bible which had one page in their language and the other in English. Tien's younger brother and sister arrived from a refugee camp and were both given accommodation in London. They asked him to join them but he was reluctant to leave because of his job. Eventually, when we found there would be better medical care for his older brother in London, he did leave and joined his relatives. We were all sorry to see him go but promised to keep in touch with one another. Tien's brother subsequently had brain surgery and this greatly improved his condition and quality of life.

Chris left language school and obtained a job in a construction company. When a flat became available in our property trust we gave him the tenancy and furnished it for him. He wanted to specialise in carpentry and enrolled at a college in London to take a diploma in the subject. While still at language school he had formed a friendship with one of the students, a very beautiful girl, the daughter of a well-known Christian who was in charge of a mission in Indonesia. Some months after he moved to London Chris phoned asking if he and his girlfriend, who was still at the language school, could come to visit. He sounded upset on the phone. When they arrived they explained that the girl's father had been told about Chris mentioning in his testimony that he had taken drugs in the past. Her father was angry with her for forming a relationship with someone who had taken drugs and banned the friendship. I was shocked that a Christian of his standing should take exception to what was past history. Chris had rarely taken drugs in Burma and certainly never touched them here. I felt this slur on his character was quite uncalled for.

This was for me an example of the damage we can do to one another when we do not forgive. Holding a record of someone's past history, a history that has been forgiven and cleansed by the blood of Christ upon the cross, seems a worse sin than the original one. Chris's girlfriend was upset as she did not want to break off their friendship. She told me she loved him and had complete trust in him. There was little I could do except plead with the father to have a more reasonable attitude. Sadly my pleas fell on deaf ears.

Minh and Anh came to visit us one evening to tell us that their company was moving to Wales and they had been asked to move with it. They were tearful at the prospect. I went to see their personnel manager and explained that although they both loved the work they did not feel ready to move away from us just yet. I explained that I thought they would consider it at a later date. The manager phoned me a week later and said that, after lengthy discussions, they were delaying the whole move especially for Minh and Anh! 'But,' he concluded, 'it will definitely take place the next year.' That spoke volumes of their dedication to their work.

Anh attended a special series of teachings on basic Christianity, then told us she wanted to be baptised. The following Sunday evening, when our extended family was gathered at our home for supper, she shared with them her decision to follow Christ. Then, to my surprise, she challenged the others to follow her example. Minh was hesitant. The Cambodian girls were interested but not ready to take that step. However, it was memorable for all of us when, a short time later, we witnessed Anh go through the waters of baptism and promise to follow the Lord Jesus Christ. How Lionel and I thanked and praised God for answering our prayers.

We had a visit from Tien. He asked if I would give him a character reference as he had applied for a place at London University to take a degree in Social Studies. Needless to say I was delighted to do so. The young man was living up to the expectations we had for him.

As Stephen was earning a good wage we advised him, in 1983, to buy a small flat, thinking that coping on his own would be good for him. He had begun a course in electronics and was getting on well. Stephen continued to write to his girlfriend and, later that year, he told us he wanted to marry her. We were very pleased and suggested that he write telling her to make plans to come to England for the wedding. We had yet to learn about Burma and the complexities of its isolationist and dictatorial government. Two months later he explained that she could not come as the government did not issue passports to nationals in these circumstances unless they first had a wedding certificate. We told Stephen he would have to consider returning to Burma if he wished to marry her. He asked me to accompany him, as he was certain there would be great opposition from his relatives to him marrying a Christian. Having very little knowledge of Burma, Lionel and I thought he was probably nervous and exaggerating the situation, and decided I should go.

I made an appointment to see the Second Secretary at the Burmese Embassy in London. The night before my appointment, a devastated Chris came to tell us that his girlfriend had been ordered to return to Indonesia and never to see him again. She had flown out of London that day. I hardly knew how to console him when I saw how badly hurt he was. The following weekend he did not come home, telling us that he was going to spend the weekend with a Buddhist family he knew from Rangoon who now lived in England. The boys had brought this couple to meet us the previous year. I disliked them, he was a boastful man and his wife chattering and empty-headed. They had a meal at our home and had openly sneered at us when Lionel said grace. We were quite pleased that

CHAPTER SIX

A HORNETS' NEST IN RANGOON

I sat and waited for over an hour at the Burmese Embassy, reading all the notices on the walls at least three times over. 'Welcome to the Golden Land', 'Visit the Land of Golden Pagodas' etc. Beautiful though the pictures were, apprehension grew within me regarding my proposed visit to Burma. Eventually a quietly spoken man tapped me on the shoulder. 'Come through,' he said and, pointing to a door along a rather shabby hall, added, 'In there.'

Entering rather nervously, I shook hands with the Second Secretary. He had our visa application forms and passports on his desk. 'We can issue you with a visa. It will take about a month. This one can't have a visa,' he said pointing to Stephen's passport.

'Why not?' I asked.

'He's changed nationality, so we don't give a visa,' he replied curtly.

'Excuse me, Sir,' I said. 'He has never changed his nationality. He was born in London and flew to Burma on a British Passport when he was three years old. Your government sent him back here because he could not pay the Foreign Resident's Card.'

'Come back next week with proof that he did not change nationality,' the Second Secretary said. 'Good bye.'

That evening I went to see Stephen to discuss how we should proceed. He looked gloomy and said I could try writing to his uncle for the necessary information but added that I did not know anything about the difficulties in his country. I wrote. A reply came from his uncle a few weeks later. He was unable to help. I asked for another appointment at the Embassy. This time I waited two hours and then was told that the Secretary had gone to the airport and wouldn't be back that day. 'Please come the same time next week,' the man at the reception desk told me. This procedure was repeated three times, but they still would not give Stephen a visa, nor was mine ready.

I decided to see my Member of Parliament because I had the papers for visa application from the Embassy and, according to their rules and regulations, British citizens were entitled to a seven day visa. My MP was most helpful. Aware of the difficulties in Burma, he advised me to register at the British Embassy on arrival should our proposed trip take place. His secretary typed a letter for me while I waited, stating that Stephen was a British citizen. As I had an appointment with the Embassy already arranged I went along with the letter and passports. Presenting the letter with the forms I waited, watching their reactions.

'Is this really from a Member of Parliament?' the Secretary said in astonishment! 'How do you know him so well?'

'He lives near us,' I replied.

Other officials came into the room and they all read the letter. 'This notepaper, is it really from the Houses of Parliament?' one official asked.

'Yes,' I replied, adding, 'There's a telephone number on it. If you have any queries, why don't you ring up?'

'Take a seat in the waiting room,' I was told. Within half an hour I was handed our passports with our visas stamped in them! We had been compelled to purchase air tickets before getting our visas as they would not consider applications without a confirmed air ticket.

We had only three weeks before we flew to Bangkok in Thailand, where we had a three day stopover before the connecting flight to Rangoon. There was just enough time to have all the necessary injections and to begin a course of antimalarial drugs. 'If I'm going to be the bridegroom's mother, I suppose I ought to have a suitable dress,' I said to Stephen. 'I need to see Ponnie first before I definitely make up my mind,' he replied. But as he bought a new suit the next day I asked the Cambodian girls to make me a dress. Stephen told me that I must wear a long skirt. Women in Burma did not wear English length skirts.

Christopher was told all about our plans and said he was glad Stephen was marrying his girlfriend. He knew Ponnie from church and was sure she was a girl of excellent character. I only wished that he could have come too, but the cost of the trip was high and we had not estimated for all the expenses that were to come.

Stephen and I arrived in the stifling heat of Bangkok airport and transferred to our hotel. I was glad to take a rest as the flight was very long and exhausting. The next day, when we took a bus into Bangkok, the relatively short distance to the city centre took one and a half-hours. Traffic jams are a major problem in that steamy, smoky, polluted city. On the way we passed several gaudily painted Buddhist Temples, swamp areas below the road level which were green and full of flies, and quaint rice straw houses built on stilts in the swamps. As we reached the city centre there were hundreds of high rise blocks of flats and luxury hotels. At the entrance to these buildings were little spirit houses where people left garlands of flowers or gifts of fruit to appease the gods that Buddhists worship.

I loved the shops. There were so many things that I had never seen before: beautiful silks in a multitude of colours and designs, exquisite sapphire, ruby and emerald jewellery, Thai lacquerware in black enamel with gold leaf patterns, and oil paintings depicting the culture of the country. Street vendors sold a variety of foods cooked over charcoal burners, some had tables laden with sweet smelling garlands of flowers for spirit worship, and others sold ebony carved elephants and jade Buddhas. There were fruit and vegetable stalls with the widest variety of produce that I had ever seen. And artists painted your portrait while you waited.

We splashed through large puddles left by recent monsoons, passed pathetic looking beggars and dodged rickshaws weaving in and out of the crowded pavements. The honking of horns and bicycle bells in the traffic laden streets made a medley of noise that was quite deafening. When we returned to the hotel, and over dinner, Stephen seemed quiet and subdued. I asked him if he was all right. 'Don't worry, Mum,' he said smiling. 'It's just difficult for me returning to my country and not knowing what will happen.' Reaching into his pocket he brought out a beautiful ring to show me. 'I bought this for Ponnie today,' he told me. 'She'll be thrilled,' I said, looking at the lovely ring. 'Tomorrow we fly to Rangoon,' I yawned. 'I'm going to have an early night. God knows the future,' I assured Stephen. 'If we put our hands into his, he will guide us and show the way. With him on our side we have nothing to fear.'

After a good night's sleep I re-packed my bags in preparation for the flight to Rangoon. It was only a short walk to the airport and we were soon boarding the Thai Airways flight for the one hour flight to Burma. From the aeroplane window I could see bright green paddy fields where rice was growing. Palms swayed in the gentle breeze and buffalos pulled carts along the dusty roads. As we flew into cloud I thought of the enormous culture shock our refugees must have undergone. Everything about this part of the world was so very different from England.

The plane landed at Mingaladon Airport, Rangoon, in the early afternoon. As we walked across the tarmac I hoped Stephen's girlfriend or her parents, Mr. and Mrs. Aung Pe, would be there to meet us. It was very hot and we took some time to go through the customs in the stuffy arrivals lounge. The formalities completed, we made our way out to where crowds of people awaited the arrivals. Searching through the faces, I hoped someone would recognise us. Then a very tall Burmese man and his petite wife came forward. They were Ponnie's parents. I had written to them before we left London suggesting that they have dinner with us at the hotel on the day we arrived.

We were greeting one another and making our way to the taxi rank when a woman in the crowd screamed loudly, 'You are not his mother! He's not going with you! Come here, Stephen, you belong to us! You go away!' The last command was directed at me! I asked Stephen who this woman was. He looked really frightened and explained she was his aunt. The woman caught hold of him and pulled him towards a waiting car.

I excused myself from Ponnie's parents and went over to the car. 'If you are taking Stephen to the hotel then I will come with you,' I insisted. 'We are together and have two rooms reserved at the Inya Lake Hotel.'

'He's not going to the hotel! He's coming with me. He belongs to us not you!' She shouted so loudly that quite a crowd gathered to watch the proceedings.

'Mrs. Maung,' I replied. 'Kindly have some sense in this situation. I've never been to Burma before and I don't speak the language. If you wish Stephen to go to your home first that is fine, but you will have to take me too.' I got into the back of the car.

Stephen's aunt kept up her long tirade all the way to the house. Our suitcases were in the car and I told the driver to leave them there when we arrived because we were going on to the Inya Lake Hotel. As the driver came into the house I assumed he was one of the family. When we were all standing in the hall Stephen's uncle came forward and introduced himself. He and Stephen spoke for a long time in Burmese, consequently I had no idea what the conversation was about. I sat down in their very well kept lounge with its highly polished teak floor and modern furnishings. Outside was a garden full of tropical flowers.

Then Stephen was taken into another room with the family. There seemed to be a lot of people in the house. I heard them all talking at length in Burmese. Darkness fell and I realised it was getting late for checking in at the hotel. Eventually the uncle came back into the lounge. 'Stephen will stay here,' he told me.

'Excuse me, Mr. Maung,' I said, 'but I have booked rooms at the Inya Lake Hotel. I wrote to you stating the purpose of this visit. It is essential that Stephen comes with me as we are having dinner with the Aung Pes tonight. Please would you arrange a taxi to take us to the hotel or maybe the driver who bought us here would like to take us.'

He called Stephen who came into the lounge looking strained. They continued to speak in Burmese for quite a long time with other family members joining in the conversation. As it was useless trying to intervene I sat down and waited for them to finish. At nine o'clock I insisted that we go to the hotel. Stephen appeared very relieved as we got into the car and drove away.

It was a very dark night with few lights and I

could see nothing of our surroundings. After we had checked into our rooms I knocked on Stephen's door. 'Come in, Mum,' he called. 'What a day! I didn't expect anything like that,' the boy sighed. 'It's late now,' he went on, 'and we won't get dinner because the dining room is shut. The Aung Pes must have gone home. Look at my room. I had forgotten how bad my country is!'

I looked around at the drab, poorly furnished bedroom. It was much the same as mine. 'What was all the conversation about?' I asked curiously.

'Oh,' he explained. 'It was pretty awful. They've got a Buddhist wedding arranged for me on Monday. They're determined to stop me marrying Ponnie and want me to marry someone I've never met before instead!'

'What!' I exclaimed in amazement, 'You're not going to have a very easy time.'

As we were both tired and still had to unpack I suggested that Stephen went to Ponnie's house after breakfast in the morning and I would get a taxi to her address about 11.30.

I returned to my room. There was only one 25 watt bulb in a small bedside lamp. The room was dim and dusty and smelt of cigarette ash. I inspected the bathroom and found that only brown water came out of the rusty taps and the toilet wasn't working. Before I undressed I took my Bible and held it near the dim lamp. My reading that day was from Isaiah, 'Fear not, for I have redeemed you; I have called you by name; you are mine. When you pass through the waters, I will be with you; and when you pass through the rivers, they will not sweep over you. When you walk through the fire, you will not be burned; the flames will not set you ablaze. For I am the Lord, your God, the Holy One of Israel, your Saviour' (Isaiah 43:1-3). These verses were God's voice to me that night. All the assurance and peace of mind that was essential if we were to survive the onslaught of the devil was there in that passage of Scripture.

As I knelt down to pray my eye fell on an enormous cockroach on the floor with what looked like long antennae that seemed to be waving at me! I hit it with my sandal but it had such a horny body that it made no impact at all. Instead the loud bang seemed to signal a horde of other cockroaches from the cracks and holes in the poor plasterwork. Surveying the scene I decided I had to learn to live with these frightening creatures – so long as they did not get into my bed!

There was a small table near the window that I had not noticed before. On it lay a dirty ashtray, a box of matches and a Gideon Bible. How pleased I was to see the Bible there. As I opened it to see if there were any addresses of local

Gideons inside, a card fell from it to the floor. Picking it up I felt a rising sense of fear. It was a tarot card with a skull and crossbones on one side and a filthy pornographic picture on the reverse. I lit a match and burnt the card in the ashtray. Getting into bed I asked God to take special care of us both in this land that was so given over to pagan worship, praying that he would guide and direct our paths in an unmistakable way. I remembered my Christian friends in England who had promised to pray for us and felt a sense of calm in the knowledge that I was surrounded by angelic care. After sleeping fitfully for a time I woke suddenly to feel the curtains flapping. My room door was open. I got up, secured the door and lock, went back into bed and dozed until dawn.

Pulling back the curtains I watched the pink sky gradually turn blue as the sun rose. It was very early but I could not rest in bed and I wanted to see my surroundings. The gardens around the hotel were pretty and well kept. There was a blaze of colour from the tropical flowers in the borders and crows cawed loudly from the trees. Beautiful large butterflies began to appear among the flowers and, as I watched this restful scene, I remembered it was Sunday and wished there was a church nearby that I could attend. Faced with an unknown future in this strange country I felt the need of some Christian fellowship to lift my spirits. I sat down by the window, read my Bible and had a time of prayer.

Feeling spiritually strengthened I decided to start the day by having a warm relaxing bath. But as I walked into the bathroom two more giant cockroaches were on the floor to meet me, and there was no plug for the bath! Turning on the tap produced no hot water at all and the toilet did not flush. I had a cold wash, dressed for the day, then went down to reception. An attractive Burmese woman said, 'Good morning, can I help you?' 'Yes,' I said. 'I arrived late last night and the toilet is not working in my bathroom. There is no plug for the bath and no hot water. Could I please change my room?' 'Yes,' she assured me. 'Sit down in reception while I make the necessary arrangements.'

There was no-one else about. The ceilings were very high and the decor loud and in clashing colours. There were large glass automatic doors leading outside. The furniture was ugly and the shabby settees did not match the paintwork. I got up to look at a glass display containing beautiful jewellery priced in kyatts. This reminded me to change some traveller's cheques as I had no local currency. The receptionist came back and said she had arranged another room which had a lovely view of the lake. But the standards were no better than the previous one except that the toilet functioned. The receptionist explained that the hot water system was out of order at the moment.

Going down to breakfast, I looked round the dull and dismal dining room. It had a very high ceiling and walls papered in dark colours. Low wattage wall lights did little to cheer it. There were only two other guests there. As I read the menu a waiter came over to tell me it was a buffet, I could help myself. The table display was rather unappetising: some papaya without the pips removed, a few slices of dry toast, small pieces of butter floating in a large bowl of cold water and a heated tray with some fried eggs on it. I helped myself to toast and spent a few minutes trying to fish a piece of butter out of the water! There were thin slices of lime to squeeze on the papaya. I added some to my plate. The waiter poured coffee made with condensed milk. I ate my breakfast and decided to go for a walk in the gardens. Although the hotel was quite large, there were only one or two cars outside and very few people about. As it was quiet and peaceful I found the walk in the gardens alongside the lake very pleasant. Because there were no buildings around us I assumed the hotel was on the outskirts of the city.

I changed some money and asked a taxi driver if he would first drive me round the city, then take me to the Aung Pes' address. We drove along good straight roads lined with palms, between buildings that needed a coat of paint. As we approached the city centre there were wide open parks and shimmering gold-domed temples everywhere. Burmese people dressed in the traditional longyis went about the streets, which had a moderate amount of traffic. All the cars were very old. In fact, it occurred to me that among them were a number of vintage cars that would fetch quite a sum of money in England. The whole place looked neglected. There was, however, something very attractive about this garden city. And the small, nicely dressed women walked gracefully about it in their pretty sarongs. When the driver pointed out the British Embassy building in Strand Road it reminded me that I had not yet registered there as advised by my MP back home.

The taxi driver dropped me at the Aung Pes' home, where a metal grill acted as a door. I banged on it and Grace Aung Pe came to greet me. Instantly I liked this charming woman. She was a little older than me, with dark long hair held in a high chignon. Her slim neat figure was dressed in a pretty sarong and she wore sandals. Her husband, who was very tall by Burmese standards, gave me a warm welcome. We sat down in a small room with a stone floor and very simple furnishings. I apologised for the change of arrangements that had been forced upon us the previous evening and asked where her

daughter was. Ponnie's mother told me Stephen
had called quite early and the two young people
had gone for a walk, arranging to meet us at a
nearby hotel for Sunday lunch.

When lunchtime came we were sitting in the
reception area of the hotel talking together when
Stephen and Ponnie came through the door. What
a lovely radiant face she had! Her long dark hair
was tied back in a ponytail. She wore her sarong
gracefully and, like her mother, she walked with
great dignity. We enjoyed our meal together.
Grace told me she would be attending the
evening service and invited me to join them. How
glad I was of this opportunity to meet with
Burmese Christians.

A large number of people were at the service
in Emmanuel Baptist Church. The pastor gave
me a warm welcome, then turned round to
conduct the choir and play the organ! He was
clearly a very talented musician, as the organ
playing and singing was of a very high standard.
The service was uplifting. Afterwards a pleasant
looking man who did not look Burmese came
over to speak to me. He introduced himself as
the Vice Consul at the British Embassy and asked
me to go to the Embassy in the morning, assuring
me that he would give me all the help that I
needed. Grace and I went with the young couple
into the pastor's office and sat down to talk.
Stephen and Ponnie asked him if he would marry

them and, as we were on a seven day visa, explained that it would have to be as soon as possible. Having decided on Wednesday at 2pm I returned to the hotel.

My first port of call on the Monday was the Embassy. The Vice Consul was most helpful and offered to stand in for Lionel at the wedding, advising me also that I would be expected to give a speech to welcome the guests and that there would be several VIPs there who would need a special welcome. He promised that he would interpret for me and see that the day ran smoothly. The Vice Consul gave me his home address and private telephone number just in case I needed to contact him out of Embassy hours. I listened carefully to his advice then discussed with him the procedure for getting Ponnie's passport and exit visa in order that she could leave with us on the Saturday. As she was a Burmese national he was not involved in the passport but gave me a list of offices that I must visit and directed us how to proceed.

Thanking him for all his help, I left and walked to the Aung Pes' home. Ponnie's father was there to meet me. 'My daughter will not be marrying Stephen as you think. I do not wish her to and my word is final. Don't think that you will succeed with her marrying Stephen or going to England, as you definitely will not.' He walked out and down the road without looking back.

Grace came towards me. 'I am so sorry,' she said, 'but he is completely against the wedding as he is a Buddhist. I don't know what to do.'

'Are you quite happy about the wedding?' I asked Grace.

'Oh yes,' she replied eagerly.

'Then,' said I, 'let us both pray that this will go forward. We are up against the powers of darkness that are arrayed against us Christians. Our God is able for every situation and he will see us through.'

We had a time of prayer in the small room and as we finished a tearful Ponnie walked in. She had been upset by her father's opposition. I assured her that God was with us and all the powers of evil would never succeed against us. Then Ponnie and I went to the Emigration Department and filled in forms in preparation for her departure on the Saturday. After she had her passport photo taken we lunched in a rather shabby restaurant.

Grace and I felt strongly that Ponnie should have a traditional white wedding dress. I assumed that in Rangoon there were twenty four hour tailors as there were in Bangkok. 'We don't have anything like that,' Grace said. 'It is difficult to buy a white wedding dress because Buddhist weddings have entirely different customs.' Remembering not being allowed to wear one myself because of the Brethren's strict rules, I puzzled over the problem. 'I've an idea,' I said eventually. 'In England we sometimes hire wedding dresses. Do you know of anyone who does that?' 'There is just one lady. She has a very small shop right the other side of the city,' Grace replied. 'Then let us take a taxi and go there straight away.'

Stephen was left to wander around the city while we made our way to the shop. When we found it, shutters covered the windows and the place looked closed. Grace banged on the shutters. 'What shall we do now?' she asked. I was just about to answer when the door was opened slightly and the lady appeared. She and Grace spoke together in Burmese and then the lady and I were introduced. When we went into a tiny room I could see no sign of dresses. The lady listened to our request. 'I only have one white dress,' she said. Ponnie tried it on. It was a beautiful dress and it fitted her perfectly. The lady said she could arrange the wedding flowers. I instructed her to make sure Ponnie had everything she needed to make her a lovely bride.

On returning to the hotel I asked to speak to the manager, wanting to explain to him that Stephen was to be married on Wednesday and I wished to arrange the reception at the hotel. I had been informed that the bridegroom's mother is responsible for the wedding in Burma! And, in a country in which tradition is held at a premium, it was important that I got things right. The manager was not available until the morning. After dinner I felt so tired, having walked round the city nearly all day in temperatures of over 90 degrees, that I decided to have an early night. In the morning the hotel manager met me in his office to discuss the wedding. After all the necessary arrangements for the reception had been made satisfactorily I then took a taxi to the Aung Pes' home.

Mr. Aung Pe greeted me and said he had been to the Tax Office where they were waiting to see me about paying the necessary government tax. He added icily, 'You will never be able to meet their demands in such a short time. It just can't be done.' I smiled warmly at him and said, 'Mr. Aung Pe, we are Christians who believe in a living God. He is the God of the impossible. I trust him and wish that you could do the same. Please come to the service tomorrow. You are Ponnie's father and we want you to be there.' Melting a little, he said he would wait and see.

I asked Grace what the payments were about. She explained that Ponnie had taken a degree at the University on a government grant. Now that an application had been made for her to leave the country, the fees had to be repaid and also some government tax. Grace accompanied me to the Tax Office where we were shown into a room with three uniformed men behind a desk.

They asked to see my passport, then confirmed what Grace had told me. Ponnie's passport could only be issued if there was a receipt for the monies and a copy of her wedding certificate.

'How much money is required?' I asked.

'Three thousand pounds,' they replied.

'I don't have three thousand pounds with me,' I told them, then asked, 'How do you expect it to be paid and where?'

'It must be paid into this account on Thursday morning, then we can issue a receipt. Provided you bring a photocopy of her wedding certificate there will be no problem with the receipt,' he assured us.

I looked around the room and noticed a Telex machine. 'May I use that? I asked, pointing to the machine. 'Yes,' one of the men replied, 'but for security reasons we must read the Telex. Have you the number that you wish to contact?' I wrote out a Telex to Lionel. 'Please transfer three thousand pounds to this account at the Myamo Foreign Economic Bank, Rangoon. Love Brenda.' No more details were allowed. 'We will contact you when there is a reply,' I was told. 'I see you are staying at the Inya Lake. Good bye.'

We had one more call to make. At the Emigration Office I was given a long questionnaire about my family. Among the questions were some I just could not answer as I had lost touch with my family. One question related to my father and mother's religion. I was tempted to write Exclusive Brethren but realised this would only confuse them! When I told Grace I did not know the address and employment of my youngest brother she looked round quickly then whispered, 'Write deceased against any you don't know the answer to!' A sense of humour was needed in these pressured circumstances. I took her advice and completed the form.

Another day was over and all I had done was fill in forms in government offices. I began to think that our bureaucracy at home was simple! As the wedding was the following day I bought two films for my camera and asked at the hotel if there was a hairdresser to do my hair. This was just being arranged when two of the tax officers came through the doors.

'Mrs. Sloggett,' one said. 'Will you come this way?' I was led into the Manager's office where they handed me a Telex from Lionel. It read, 'How are you getting on? What is Burma like? Is the hotel nice? Why do you want so much money? Are you going on a spending spree? Give Stephen and Ponnie my love and, if they are getting married, tell me when. Love Lionel.' The officers watched me reading, then said, 'You must reply immediately. You can use the Telex here. Write the message down and we will send it for you. Be careful what you say.' I wrote,

CHAPTER SEVEN

OPPOSITION

Stephen and Ponnie's wedding service went well. We were all especially pleased to see Ponnie's father there. After the service the young couple and their guests adjourned to the hotel, to a jade room in which two small white settees stood together on a platform. The newly weds sat on one while Grace and I sat on the other. The male guests were very colourful in their best longyis and white jackets. And the ladies were resplendent in their beautiful sarongs. The Vice Consul guided the speeches and interpreted for me even though a large number of the guests spoke English very well. It had been a compulsory subject in Burma under British rule but the military dictatorship had since banished it from schools. A room adorned with bouquets of red roses was prepared for the bride and bridegroom at the hotel. I had brought two suitcases with me from England as these are difficult to obtain in Burma. One of them was left in the room for Ponnie to pack her belongings for the flight to Bangkok on the Saturday.

The day after the wedding Grace and I went to the Emigration Office where we were told that Lionel's money had been paid into the Tax

Account. A receipt was issued and we went to the Passport Office. There we handed in the completed forms and were told that Ponnie's passport would be ready to collect the next day. That attended to, I spent the afternoon visiting the Shwedagon Pagoda. This, one of the Seven Wonders of the World, is an enormous Buddhist Temple with a massive dome coated with tons of pure gold. For hundreds of years, in an attempt to have their sins pardoned, the people have bought gold leaf which the temple priests melt down over the golden dome. In the bright sunshine it is a quite spectacular sight. I walked barefoot around the marble floors and watched people chanting in front of the numerous gods and offering flowers and fruit to the idols.

As I read my Bible that evening and thought of the price paid for my redemption, I thanked the Lord for being my substitute and for bearing the penalty of my sin on the cross. The Christian faith stands alone, totally distinct from all other religions. Our message is one that elevates man: God reaching down in his great love to man to lift him up to a new life. Other religions are man in all his sinfulness trying to reach up to a god who demands constant appeasement. For Christians the price has been paid, the debt cancelled. Christ sets us free, not to do as we like, but to serve him.

There was one more day before we were to

leave this fascinating city, and we had things to do in it. When Grace and I called at the passport office the clerk told us that a few more enquiries still had to be made, but that they were not of any consequence. Ponnie's passport, we were assured, would be to hand in time for the 4pm flight to Bangkok. Grace then took me to the Scott Market to see all the Burmese crafts. I admired the delicate silverware and bought two oil paintings. They were of a high standard and would serve to remind me of my visit.

There were many beggars in the market: young mothers with very sick children, their bodies covered in sores; pathetic old blind men and elderly women dressed in rags. As we walked along the roads we saw Buddhist priests with their shaved heads and saffron robes going from door to door with begging bowls. My mind went to one of the psalms. 'I was young and now am old, yet I have never seen the righteous forsaken or their children begging bread. They are always generous and lend freely; their children will be blessed' (Psalm 37:25-26).

Grace, who saw Ponnie's move to England as part of God's good plan for her daughter, said she would come to the airport the following day. It helped that the steam seemed to have gone out of her husband's opposition now that his daughter was married. We said goodbye and I returned to the hotel. I greatly admired this small, determined woman, she had such strong firm faith. And I hoped that now Ponnie was Stephen's wife, there would be a new strength and stability brought into his life. Ponnie was so like her mother.

The telephone rang in my room as I was changing for dinner. It was Stephen. 'My uncle and aunt have phoned,' he told me. 'They want to make up with us now and are sorry they didn't come to the wedding! Uncle wants us all to go there for dinner tonight.'

'Very well,' I said, 'but I'm tired and I'd prefer to stay here and have an early night. You go by all means,' I added.

'They asked especially that you come too as they want to get to know you,' said Stephen.

'All right,' I agreed wearily. 'Just arrange a taxi for us and give me a few minutes to dress.'

We were welcomed at his uncle's home but, as before, Stephen and Ponnie were taken to a room in the back of the house and I was left in the front room with him. He put the television on for me and went to pour some drinks.

When he came back with a tumbler full of whisky I protested politely. 'I don't drink like that and, as I am very thirsty in the heat, could I please have some lemonade?' He brought a glass but I only drank a small amount as it was strong.

For a while the man talked amicably. Then he said, 'You know the passport isn't ready?'

'Yes,' I replied, adding, 'but I am told it will be to hand for the flight tomorrow.'

'There is no chance of it being to hand. If you want my help I will give it, but I shall want two thousand pounds.'

'I leave tomorrow and I do not have that amount with me,' I told him firmly. 'But even if I had, that represents a bribe and I am not prepared to bribe.'

'You will regret that decision,' he said quietly.

Just then his wife came into the room with our dinners. 'Can't I eat with the family tonight?' I asked. 'It would give me an opportunity to meet them.' 'No,' Stephen's uncle replied. 'They have had theirs. You and I will dine together.' I sat down. Observing that my meal was different to his I commented on the fact. He replied that he was a diabetic, something I already knew from the boys. So, feeling very hungry, I ate my meal in silence. There was an unpleasant atmosphere in the room that disturbed me. When Stephen and Ponnie reappeared, I told them we needed to leave as it was late. Ponnie looked upset and I thought she had been crying. In the taxi to the hotel I asked her what was wrong. 'They told me I'm ugly and that they didn't know why Stephen married me,' she said tearfully. I reassured her as best I could.

I had just finished packing when I suddenly grew cold and shivery. Thinking it might be a reaction to the week's events, I got into bed. Then violent pains seized me and I ran to the bathroom. After two hours of severe vomiting I fainted on the floor. Coming round some time later, I looked at my watch in the dim light. It was 3.30am. As I tried to get back into bed the terrible pain seized me again. I had never felt so ill in my life. My head felt as if it would burst and the room spun round about me. The next time I looked at my watch it was 6.30am. Picking up the phone, I rang reception. 'Would you please get a doctor,' I said, as insistently as I could. 'I'm ill and my flight leaves this afternoon.'

Before long two nurses and a doctor came into my room. Having examined me the doctor said, 'I must admit you straight away to the hospital.' 'No,' I replied, on my tour of Rangoon I had seen the hospital, and it was far worse than the hotel. 'If I need a drip, set it up here.' He did. I remember nothing more until six that evening when I looked at my watch. I was horrified. 'I've missed my flight and my visa expires today,' I told the doctor who was still with me. 'Would you please write a note to say that I am ill and can't fly?' I had been told that remaining in the country after my visa expired carried an automatic prison sentence. Having written the note, he left me in the charge of a nurse, saying he would see me in the morning. The room spun about me and everything went black. At one point I thought I saw Stephen and Ponnie in my room. She prayed silently at my bedside.

The night passed and in the morning the nurse left my room to get some breakfast. My address book was on the bedside table. I telephoned the Vice Consul at his home and he assured me he would take charge of the situation. Because everything shut on Sundays I was quite safe for the next few hours. First thing on Monday morning he would arrange an Embassy car to collect me and take me to the Embassy. I was too ill that day to bother about anything and spent it dozing between bouts of pain. Monday morning came and I felt a little stronger. I tried to dress before the Embassy car came. I had almost succeeded when dizziness forced me to lie down. A knock indicated the arrival of my transport, and kindly hands packed my case and helped me to the car. As we left the hotel I caught sight of Stephen and Ponnie getting into a car behind mine. They had not left either.

Once at the Embassy the Vice Consul arranged two easy chairs into a bed for me and called out a Canadian doctor. She was a bright cheerful woman who told me I was unfit to travel for a week! I asked her what had caused this upset but she did not know. As I had no fever, infection seemed to be ruled out. The doctor quizzed me in great detail about what I had eaten. Later that day the Vice Consul returned. 'I've been unable to get the necessary stay permit for seven days,' he told me. 'The Immigration Department has refused permission. They'll only give one for twenty-four hours, and for that I'm afraid twenty passport photos are needed. There's a photo shop nearby. I'll come with you in the car and get them taken.'

Feeling faint and sick I managed to get to the photographer, then from there to the Immigration Office. 'You must leave Rangoon tomorrow on Burma Airways,' the official said sternly.

'I've a return ticket on Thai Airways and I know there is a scheduled flight on Thursday. Surely it makes sense for me to use my ticket?'

'We can't do that because you are permitted to stay only until tomorrow. The same rule applies to Stephen. His wife can't accompany him as there are a number of matters to be cleared on her passport.'

My heart sank on hearing this news, but I was too weak to protest. Embassy staff helped me back into my hotel room for the night and took Stephen and me to the airport the next day. Ponnie and Grace waved their sad goodbyes as we boarded an old Fokker aeroplane for Bangkok.

My room in the Airport Hotel was like a palace compared to the room in Rangoon. As we had two days until our flight to London I rested by the swimming pool, gathering strength for the long flight home. Thinking of the opposition this Christian marriage had met confirmed to me the words of a retired overseas missionary at the boys' language school. 'Buddhism is a stronghold of Satan. If anyone is converted to Christianity from this, there are always powers of opposition that cannot be met by our human methods.' Ephesians 6:12 says, 'For our struggle is not against flesh and blood, but against the rulers, against the authorities, against the powers of this dark world and against the spiritual forces of evil in the heavenly realms.'

I had underestimated the depth of the opposition. However, despite that, I felt that Stephen and Ponnie's marriage would survive all the difficulties it would meet. They had taken their vows seriously before God and he would bring them through to victory. I remembered his voice to me the first night I spent in Rangoon, 'Fear not, for I have redeemed you; I have called you by name; you are mine' (Isaiah 43:1).

CHAPTER EIGHT

JOY AND SADNESS

On arriving home I made an appointment to see my doctor as the attacks of pain and dizziness continued. Extensive tests showed no infection and he told me he suspected some form of food poisoning. It was two months before I felt really well. During that time Minh and Anh were preparing to move to Wales. They had saved enough money for a deposit and were buying their own home. Their company gave them a cash sum as an added incentive to move. The Cambodian girls went to London for interviews for better jobs working for a London designer. My extended family was learning to be independent and I felt proud of their achievements.

Lionel came home one evening with bad news. The manager of our property department had told him that Christopher had left his flat, giving no forwarding address. I was really upset about this and went to see if Stephen knew of his whereabouts. As I expected he did not know where Chris had gone, and he was very low in spirits himself because his wife was still in Burma. I promised to go to the Burmese Embassy to see what was happening to Ponnie. When I went I was told that her passport would be issued when the government was satisfied with enquiries they were making. I asked what the enquiries were, as I had been told in Rangoon that they had all been completed. 'We can only say that it may take a year to issue the passport. We need to hold a deposit here for her return air fare.'

When Lionel and I discussed these problems he agreed to pay the deposit to the Embassy and told me to write to the Vice Consul in Rangoon. Grace replied. As Ponnie was a Burmese national, until the passport was issued the Embassy was not involved. The Tax Office, she told me, required further sums of money. After several demands I contacted the Foreign Office for advice. They said they had heard of situations like this and if they intervened there could be repercussions for the family. We were advised to pay up before the sum escalated to a price we could not consider.

A letter arrived from Grace telling us that her husband had collapsed in the street outside their home and was dead on arrival at the hospital. She was now without any means of support, she told us, yet although her three younger children were still at home, she was experiencing daily the reality of the Bible promise, 'My God will meet all your needs according to his glorious riches in Christ Jesus' (Philippians 4:19). I thought of Ponnie in Rangoon: perhaps in God's wisdom she had remained there to comfort her mother in her bereavement.

Minh and Anh bought a three bedroomed house in Wales. I went to visit them and was delighted to hear they were both attending the local Baptist Church. When I asked if they had heard any news of Hai as I still prayed for him, Minh shook his head sadly.

Stephen's faith began to falter as the months passed and there was no news of Ponnie coming. He went through a period of dark depression. It was a difficult time for all of us, but we were aware that this ministry to our refugee family had both good times and bad. When we could not see the end of the road we had to trust the wisdom of our heavenly Father. I thought again of my early experiences when walking in the valley of the shadow of death. The Lord had walked with me then. And when I felt discouraged I remembered his voice in the night, 'It is I, be not afraid.' Those words were said to the disciples when they were in the boat on a storm-tossed sea and it was night. They spoke to us in our stormy times, and in our times of darkness and difficulty.

I was picking daffodils in the front garden one bright spring morning in 1984 when the post van drew up. The postman got out and asked me to sign for a registered letter. It was from the

British Embassy in Rangoon. Ponnie's passport had been issued, her entry visa for the United Kingdom was being processed and the Burmese authorities requested that I accompany her to London as she had never flown before. Stephen was delighted! I began to make my travel arrangements. As I did not wish to return to Burma, I suggested that I meet her flight at Bangkok. Having read many reports of the thousands of Cambodian refugees in border camps, I decided to make this journey worthwhile by visiting one of the camps. I liaised with the Burmese Embassy over Ponnie's flight details and finally left London in April to bring her home.

The refugee camps on the Thai-Cambodian border stretched for miles and housed hundreds of thousands of homeless and destitute people who had been forced to leave their homes in Cambodia when Pol Pot ravaged the land. Southeast Asian Outreach was working in the Pen Parat Nithorn Camp, and it was there I had the privilege of seeing the level of practical Christian care that was extended to them through the various Christian relief agencies. Southeast Asian Outreach had a programme of nutrition and supplementary feeding, an agricultural programme and organised adult literacy classes in the camps. Their nurses assisted in health projects, working alongside other agencies, e.g.

World Vision, which had skilled medical teams caring for the sick and injured.

The good news of the gospel spread among the refugees and there were daily accounts of hundreds giving their lives to Christ. In these tragic circumstances we saw the triumph of the cross of Christ as needy people came to know him as the Light of the World. He is indeed the only hope in a world of strife, warfare, famine and man's inhumanity to his fellow man.

I was sitting in the lounge of the airport hotel watching the flight indicators for the arrival time of Ponnie's flight from Burma. Having brought with me Helen Penfold's book, *Remember Cambodia*, I settled down to read it when the indicator board said there was a one hour delay. Paul and Helen Penfold founded Southeast Asian Outreach with a Cambodian Christian, Chirac Taing, who came to England and asked Christians here to pray for his country. When he returned home he was one of the first Cambodian martyrs to die for Christ. After reading for a while I looked up and noticed a very well dressed man sitting nearby also watching the flight indicator. He was very distressed and kept wiping away tears. After discreet observation I was puzzled. He looked of Cambodian origin, but how could there be anyone from Cambodia, well dressed and in the airport hotel lounge? He certainly did not look like one of the 300,000 refugees in the Thai-Cambodian border camps, some of whom were being granted political asylum in Western countries.

Curiosity got the better of me. 'Excuse me, sir, but are you all right?' I enquired quietly.

'No, not really. I'm very upset. My country ... it's all so terrible.' He spoke very disjointedly.

'Could you tell me your nationality?' I asked.

'Why?' he replied, looking round in an agitated manner. 'Do you know me then?'

'No,' I admitted. 'But I'd guess you are Cambodian.'

'How could you know that? No-one knows about Cambodia and no-one cares. It's terrible. I've just come back from the borders and the fighting continues.'

'Yes,' I agreed, 'I know, but there are those who do care.'

He looked surprised and asked about me. I told him I was a Christian and that there were Christians in England who cared. When I showed him the book I was reading he asked to borrow it. As I hadn't finished reading it myself, I refused. The flight indicator showed that his flight was being called. Giving me his card, he asked me to send him a copy of the book. I promised to do so and gave him our address card.

As the Burma Airways flight had landed I went to the arrivals lounge. Ponnie came through looking apprehensive and a little bewildered. I ran to greet her. We went to the hotel together and I took her to my room. She told me about her family and I asked how her mother was. When Ponnie unpacked her case she handed me a present from Grace. It was an exquisite jewel box with an intricate design in gold leaf. Inside was a silver necklace, earrings and a bracelet in the delicate work that I had so admired in the Scott Market.

A very strong bond had grown between Grace and me during that difficult week we spent together. Now she was a widow I knew she must be included in that verse from James' Epistle, 'To look after orphans and widows' (1:27). Ponnie and I went shopping in Bangkok the next day where I bought her some western style clothes. We thoroughly enjoyed the time together and I began to love my new daughter-in-law. As we were to catch the midnight flight from Bangkok to London, we packed our purchases and had our last meal together in Thailand.

Because the weather had turned very cold and there were flurries of snow in the air, Lionel bought a sheepskin coat for Ponnie to wear on her first day in England. We drove Stephen and his new bride to their flat and told him to take good care of her as she adjusted to our climate. In the evening Lionel called me into the study to enquire how my trip had gone. As he looked very troubled, I asked what was wrong before telling him of my travels. 'Well,' he sighed. 'Ponnie is here now and we have completed what I felt God wanted us to do. But the costs have far exceeded our income.' Lionel showed me a bank statement. I was shocked. 'Why didn't you tell me about this earlier?' I asked. 'I knew you would be worried and I thought you might have pulled out of the commitment,' he replied. We discussed how to solve the problem and decided to sell our house and move to a cheaper area.

In May 1984 we put our house on the market at a very high price as we did not want to sell it before we had another property lined up. We had seen plans of new houses being built on an estate near Reading. They were nice, but they were not scheduled to be completed until the end of the year. But finding a house was not all that was on our minds. We were still very concerned about Chris, having been told that he had gone to the South Coast and made friends with the Burmese family he knew from his Rangoon days. There was little we could do about this distressing situation, but I felt strongly that the enemy of our souls was using this to try to drive him back from his Christian commitment.

When the battle is on we need to wear the right armour if we are to defeat the enemy. How often we fail in this, even though the words from the Apostle Paul are there to guide us. I was not fully in the gain of this teaching myself, as circumstances were to prove. 'Put on the full armour of God, so that when the day of evil comes, you may be able to stand your ground, and after you have done everything, to stand. Stand firm then, with the belt of truth buckled around your waist, with the breastplate of righteousness in place, and with your feet fitted with the readiness that comes from the gospel of peace. In addition to all this, take up the shield of faith, with which you can extinguish all the flaming arrows of the evil one. Take the helmet of salvation and the sword of the Spirit, which is the word of God' (Ephesians 6:13-17).

It was a great surprise to us when our house sold the first week it was on the market, particularly as our new home near Reading was not due to be finished for six months. A short lease on a furnished house was a necessity. I felt very sad at leaving our lovely home in its quiet Buckinghamshire village. I had no idea that events would lead to such a drastic course of action. However, we had had such definite confirmation that this call to assist homeless people was God's will for us that we knew we must trust God to work out all our circumstances.

As we were about to leave our home in Burnham the telephone rang. I could not work out who the caller was. With the work and stress of moving I had completely forgotten the episode at the airport hotel. Suddenly I remembered. This was the Cambodian man I'd met for a short time in Bangkok. Mr. Kong said he was coming to London and, having read *Remember Cambodia*, he wanted to meet Paul and Helen Penfold. I told him we were moving, gave him the telephone number of the rented house in Maidenhead, then rang off.

Our furniture went into storage and we tried to settle in our new home. The decor was drab and depressing and the house was on a busy and noisy road. I needed to remember this was only a temporary situation but, with interrupted sleep, I felt increasingly tired and drained. Both of us felt depressed at leaving Burnham, particularly the church in which we had found a spiritual home.

The telephone rang one morning. It was Mr. Kong. He was in London for a week and wanted to meet Helen Penfold and myself. He suggested we meet at one of London's top hotels. I was amazed, and somewhat concerned, that this 'refugee' should be living in such style. Southeast Asian Outreach had helped some influential Cambodian people to start a new life in London and Paris, but generally they lost their wealth when they left Cambodia. After a long conversation with Helen, we agreed that with her husband, Paul, we would meet him.

Following tea in his hotel, Paul and Helen asked Mr. Kong about his background. He told us in an agitated way that he had been a senior politician in one of the many governments before Pol Pot. When Pol Pot came to power, and the Khmer Rouge took control of the capital city, they had confiscated his home and killed his wife and two sons. He and three others had escaped by helicopter, then flown out of the country. Mr. Kong talked for a long time. Paul and Helen told him that a fellow countryman of his, Mr. C, was also in London. This man, they explained, had paid a huge sum to get his relatives out of Cambodia into safety. Mr. Kong telephoned Mr. C and arranged to meet him at his house after we had dined at his club which was, he told us, just a short walk away. Imagine our consternation when his club turned out to be a Casino Club! 'What would my father say if he saw me now!' I asked Helen who, like me, saw the funny side of our situation.

We dined sumptuously and then he asked us to join him at the gaming tables. While he played, we discussed whether Mr. Kong's story could be true. Paul and Helen were fairly sure it was. We would take an opportunity, they decided, to discuss the book and see if he had any interest in Christianity. When he returned he laughed and said, 'Well, I lost £30,000. Never mind, I will win it back later.' I had never heard anything like it before and reacted angrily. 'If you have £30,000 to lose, why don't you spend your money on something worthwhile? You said that you are concerned about your country and the refugees in exile. Don't you know most of them are in dire poverty and have difficulty in getting jobs? Yet you live like this and do nothing to help. Why don't you set up some business venture so they can earn a respectable living? I've got plenty of suggestions I could put to you.'

Mr. Kong said he was sorry, and he did look upset for a while. Then he called his chauffeur, announcing that it was time to visit Mr. C. We all got into his silver Mercedes and drove to Eltham where we received a very warm welcome. Among the photographs Mr. C had on the wall were some of himself with King Sihanouk. Next morning Helen and I had a long talk. She and her husband had checked out some of Mr. Kong's details and confirmed that his story was true. However, we all agreed that we needed to be very careful in our dealings with this man.

We had one further meeting with Mr. Kong when he said he was seriously considering setting up a business venture for refugees. He also seemed interested in the Christian faith. I told Thida and Boppha about him but they were not impressed. 'Be careful, Mum,' Thida cautioned. 'Those leaders in Cambodia are usually bad men.' I should have paid far more attention to her warning.

CHAPTER NINE

A FEARFUL FRACAS

One day Mr. Kong phoned three times from Milan, telling us he was just about to leave for Holland. Then another call came through from Zurich, where he said he would be a few days. He phoned twice more that evening, saying he wanted to stay a night at our home to discuss his countrymen in exile. At the end of that week he called from Heathrow Airport asking me to pick him up. As I was preparing dinner, Lionel drove to the airport and collected him. Over our meal I watched Mr. Kong with growing alarm. He was extremely disturbed and spoke very rapidly. Mr. Kong told us he had a villa in Marbella, Spain, and wanted us to join him there for a holiday. When Lionel said he was busy and could not get away, our guest looked at me and suggested I went with him. Having elaborated on the luxurious lifestyle he had at the villa, he pressed his invitation. I refused. Looking him straight in the eye, I said, 'No, thank you. I will not go to the Marbella. Actually I don't like it.'

As he had indicated an interest in setting up a business venture to help the refugees, I asked him what he was thinking of doing. He laughed at me. 'You work too hard,' he said. 'You need a holiday. Come to Spain with me and I will give you a good holiday.' I told him very firmly that I would not go.

Suddenly Mr. Kong raised his arm and gave Lionel a karate chop across the back of his neck. My husband landed on the floor and his glasses fell off. Mr. Kong trod on them, then, picking up a bottle of wine from the sideboard, he hit Lionel with it. Horrified, I ran into the kitchen to fetch the proverbial rolling pin! I screamed at Mr. Kong to stop attacking Lionel but he only grew more violent. Alison, who had been upstairs, ran down in fright. 'Phone the police,' I shouted, 'Dial 999.' She did. Mr. Kong then turned on me with the broken bottle. I hit him with the rolling pin to stave off the attack, knocking the bottle out of his hand. There was broken glass, spilt wine and blood everywhere. 'Get out!' I screamed at the man. To my relief the police were there to arrest him as he tried to leave. 'Stay in the house,' an officer told us as they packed Mr. Kong into their car. 'We'll be back.'

I returned to the lounge where Lionel sat, dazed and shocked. Thankfully he was not badly injured, sustaining only cuts and some heavy bruising. In the scuffle I had deliberately kicked Mr. Kong's briefcase under the settee. Pulling it out, I read some of the papers inside. To my horror they involved supplying arms to the military wing of a political party in Cambodia. I had heard of this group. They were one of the many to take up arms against Pol Pot.

The police returned and questioned us about the situation. I gave them his briefcase and told them Mr. Kong was dangerous and should not be allowed to come freely to Britain. They had not even heard of Cambodia and seemed uninterested in what I had to say. When I asked what would happen to Mr. Kong, we were told he would be held in custody overnight and charged with assault in the morning. Having looked round the room, and taken Mr. Kong's briefcase, they explained that no charges would be made against us. Then came the bombshell. Because Mr. Kong had a cut that needed a few stitches, one of the policemen explained, he could make a private charge of assault against me. I was horrified. Severely shocked, we silently began to clean up the terrible mess. Alison, who had left for work immediately after phoning for help, was thankfully spared this distressing sight.

In the morning I went to see our solicitor. I was extremely frightened that Mr. Kong would come back, as he was only charged with a breach of the peace, fined and released. Our solicitor asked to see Mr. Kong's card. He had heard of the man, and he warned me that if he pursued a case against me it could cost many thousands of pounds. He had money to burn. 'What should I do?' I asked. Knowing we were shortly moving to a new house he said, 'You must literally get lost. Don't give your new address to anyone you can't trust implicitly. Go ex-directory, no calls offered, and don't accept any post that could come from him.'

Lionel and I were appalled at this episode, realising with hindsight that we had been unwise to allow Mr. Kong into our home. I had not paid enough attention to Thida's warning. We took the whole matter to the Lord, asking for his forgiveness for our mistakes and protection from further developments. A week later the postman rang the doorbell. I answered it and was handed a registered envelope with a Spanish stamp.

'Do I have to receive this?' I asked, feeling sick and faint.

'Why?' the man asked. 'Are you in trouble, dear? You look as pale as a ghost?'

'Yes, I am. Can you help me?' I asked. 'Step inside I want to steam it open.'

He kindly agreed to allow me to do that. It was indeed a private summons of assault against me. I dried the envelope stuck it down and wrote, 'Not known at this address.' Handing it back to the postman, I was relieved to learn that it would be returned to Spain. I explained to him that we were leaving the next day and giving no forwarding address. All post for us could be destroyed. That was a sad end to a sad episode. May God forgive me my foolishness.

When we moved into our new house we only notified very close friends and relatives. Every time the phone rang or there was a knock at the door I felt sick with apprehension. Our solicitor informed me that Mr. Kong had a year to lodge his case. If he failed to do so in that time the matter was closed.

We had ex-Exclusive Brethren friends at Argyle Chapel, the church we joined. I could not bring myself to tell anyone except them what had happened. Our friends shared it with one of the elders, an extremely kind and caring man. They visited us and prayed with us that we would be protected from further harm and that we would know God's peace in our home. An awful black depression came on me and, feeling guilty and despairing, I told Lionel that I would never again become involved in Christian work because what had happened disqualified me. Seeing how low I was, he arranged for our daughter to book a holiday for us in Kenya. He thought the holiday and a safari would do me good. I looked forward to the break, thinking that three weeks away from all the stress and strain was just what we needed.

On arriving in Nairobi, we checked into the Norfolk Hotel, then contacted Gideon friends who were members of the Nairobi Branch. Gerald and Beatrice Njoroge invited us to dinner and our first evening in Kenya was spent enjoying their fellowship and warm hospitality. Gerald, who has since died, was a dental surgeon who also lectured in the Dental School of Nairobi University. Beatrice is a Health Development Officer with a Christian mission which is involved in primary health care. As well as having two children of their own, the Njoroges adopted two orphans.

When I got up early the following morning to dress for the safari, Lionel looked at me and said in a shocked voice, 'Look in a mirror. What's wrong with you?' Although I felt well I discovered I was covered in a red rash. 'Nothing to worry about,' I assured him. 'But I'll arrange with the manager to see a doctor just to confirm I'm all right for the safari.' A taxi took me to the Nairobi Hospital where a doctor told me the rash was caused by an allergy. He gave me an antihistamine and I returned to the hotel feeling fine. But when I sat down to breakfast I suddenly felt very ill, and everything went black.

When I regained consciousness I could hear people speaking to me but I could not see. I tried to answer but no words came. Gradually my sight and speech came back. Some days later, when Lionel visited me in hospital, I asked him what had happened. He explained that I collapsed unconscious at the hotel and was rushed to hospital where the doctors could find no recordable heartbeat and that for several hours they battled to save my life. I had an appalling rash from head to foot. The horrible blisters were even in my hair! Not finding any cause for the acute anaphylactic shock, the doctor had given me steroids intravenously. That, I realised, explained the drip.

I was in hospital for a week during which Gerald and Beatrice, with great care and compassion, visited me daily. They prayed for my recovery. Gerald, despite his busy life, even made time to show Lionel some of the sights of Nairobi. Their daily visits were so special that I shall never forget their kindness. When my condition was under control, I was flown home and admitted to hospital at Windsor. My recovery was slow, but I realised that I needed to be laid aside for a time to experience the company of the Lord and to know again the touch of his loving hand restoring me to health and wholeness. I read my Bible and was encouraged to learn how wonderfully God restores those who have failed, and in his mercy and loving kindness even uses their failures and mistakes, turning them to good. As I trusted him afresh and the year drew to a close, so my fear of Mr. Kong left me.

CHAPTER TEN

RESTORATION AND
A NARROW ESCAPE

Neither Lionel nor I liked Reading and, although we were cared for extremely well at Argyle Chapel Assembly, we didn't feel at home. Because my husband wanted to start a business on his own, he decided to sell his shares in the property trust. The rearrangement of our affairs allowed us to consider moving back to Burnham. It was a time of change, both for us and within our extended family. Thida was married in London and we all enjoyed her wedding. Stephen and Ponnie came to the wedding. It was so rewarding to see the good influence Ponnie had in her husband's life. He was getting on very well in his work in electronics and they were considering moving to a house as their flat was rather small. Our younger daughter, Alison, got engaged and we really liked Russell, our future son-in-law.

One cold December day we took a walk in Burnham as both of us wanted to return there. We noticed bricks outside a house not far from our old home. On making enquiries at the estate agent, we discovered that there were plans to build five houses. One of them was just what we were looking for. It had all we needed, even a large games room which my husband could use as an office. As our house in Reading sold easily, in God's great goodness we were able to return to Burnham less than two years after we had left it. Our new home was beautiful and we soon had the garden laid out to our liking.

October 1986 was a happy month and we had a glorious warm sunny day for our daughter's wedding. Alison looked beautiful in the lovely wedding dress Thida made for her. It had taken three months to sew little pearls into the dress's silk embroidered organza. Rosemary looked wonderful in a dress of apricot-watermarked taffeta, another of Thida's creations.

Minh and Anh went to America for a holiday and visited Hai's wife and four children while they were there. Hai's two eldest children were studying at university. Minh was upset when he learned that his sister-in-law had grown used to life without Hai and that she was seeking a divorce from him. She had made a great success of her life in America over the eleven years she had been there, as was evidenced by her nice home and Cadillac. Minh had a sister who was resettled in San Jose. When he visited her, he asked her to apply for Hai to go to the States. He was rightly concerned that Hai's children should recognise their father and have opportunity of getting to know him again. When Minh told me this on his return from holiday, I could see how much it meant to him.

I spent a very happy weekend with Minh and Anh in their new home in Wales. They told me they both wanted to go to America to be near their relatives. While I could quite understand this, I felt sad at the thought of them leaving. Six months later we all gathered at the airport to see them leave Britain to begin a new life in the States. I promised Anh we would come and visit her when she had found a home of her own. They kept in touch with us and we were pleased to hear that they were just as quickly employed and settled in a comfortable flat in America as they had been when they came to England.

About that time Stephen told me that Christopher had married the divorced daughter of their Burmese acquaintance. Chris's father-in-law had arranged for his daughter to visit England from Burma on a holiday visa and he needed a British citizen to marry her in order that she could stay here. While I was dismayed at this news, I wrote to Chris to say we would be glad to see him. I had a feeling that this marriage would never work as I had heard about this girl from Grace in Rangoon. Grace wrote regularly, and I knew from her letters that she had been very ill. Conditions in Burma were getting worse and there was little by way of medical care for the average citizen.

Lionel and I flew to America for a holiday and called to see Minh and Anh in Texas. What a loving welcome we had in their home. Minh asked if we would go to see his sister-in-law. He hoped that we might persuade her to accept her husband back. When we flew to San Antonio and met Hai's family, his four children received us warmly but his wife distanced herself from us. When we discussed the possibility of him going to America she grew quite hostile. She had made a very good life for herself in America, she told us. It was over eleven years since she had left Vietnam, and she wished to put the whole of her past behind her. Lighting a candle in a small Buddhist shrine in the room she said, 'Buddha has helped me. I don't need Christians. You can tell my husband he will not come to America.'

On our return to Minh and Anh's home, they asked me if I would tell Hai that his wife would never accept him and that divorce was imminent. 'What dreadful news to tell him,' I exclaimed. 'It's surely better that you break it to him.' Minh looked at me sadly. 'Mom, you have such faith in God,' he said. 'We believe you could help him in this dilemma. We'll apply for him to come to America, but his application would be greatly helped if you supported it.' 'How can I do that as I live in England? I asked.

Anh had spent many hours in the refugee

department that was relevant to Hai's case and she showed me the forms that went to the Orderly Department Programme in Bangkok. They needed a third signatory, someone who would vouch for both the truth of the documents and Minh and Anh's promise to care for Hai. I read them all carefully and told them that I wished to take the whole matter to the Lord. Having prayed with Minh and Anh, we left America. I had a great burden for Hai, and I prayed that in his sad circumstances he would be led to Christ.

Soon after arriving back in England we had a reunion for our extended family. Christopher came with his wife. Tien, his wife and new baby daughter were there as well, as were Thida, her husband and Boppha. Tien was now half way through his University course and although he found it hard he was making good progress. Ponnie had obtained a very good job as a food analyst with an American Company. It was lovely to have them together and they were all interested in our photographs of Minh and Anh in America.

We maintained close links with Southeast Asian Outreach and were particularly interested in Mark and Angela Timmins who were church planting in Thailand near the Cambodian borders. Having prayed for Hai daily, in 1987 Lionel and I felt it was right for me to go to Vietnam to see him. Because of my experience when applying for a Burmese visa, I was nervous when I went to the Vietnamese Embassy in London. After telling the officials there of my involvement with refugees in this country, I said that I wished to visit Vietnam to see the eldest brother of two of them. When they asked me the reason for my interest I told them I was a Christian and that Christ's love was the motivation for my work and not political ideology.

The two Vietnamese officials seemed very interested in the work and asked me many questions about my faith. I explained that I wished to take a small tape recorder and my camera with me so that Hai could record messages for his family and I could take some photographs for them. The Embassy officials gave me visa application forms to complete and the address of an agent who would make the necessary travel arrangements. As I left the Embassy one of the officials told me, 'You will not be allowed to visit homes but you will be allowed to see Hai at the hotel.' I thanked them for their kind help, then went to the Burmese Embassy to apply for a visa as we decided that I should have a weekend with Grace in Rangoon. Stephen had introduced me to an elder in the church in Rangoon and I hoped to be able to accept his invitation to visit his church. This time I was well received at the Embassy and there were no difficulties.

I flew to Bangkok and met Mark and Angela. It was a great privilege to learn more about the work they were doing for Southeast Asian Outreach and how the Lord was blessing it. Because the area they worked in was staunchly Buddhist they experienced a lot of opposition. But God was adding believers to his Church through their ministry.

Having attended a service in the Bangkok Evangelical Church just before flying to Vietnam, I was wondering if I could go to a church service in Saigon. A young American man shook hands with me as I left the church. 'What are you doing here?' he asked. I told him about the work of Southeast Asian Outreach, then said I was going to Vietnam before spending a weekend in Burma. 'Vietnam?' he queried. I explained about my mission to see Hai, who had spent ten years in prison as a former Naval Commander. 'He's out of prison now?' he asked, sounding surprised. 'Yes,' I assured him, then went on, 'I visited his wife in the States and she has got a divorce.' 'He's one of the few high ranking officers to be released,' the young man said. 'You see,' he continued, 'I know quite a lot about Vietnam because my father worked in the American Embassy and I lived in Saigon myself for several years. It's very difficult now. You won't find the visit easy. Let me have your name and I will pray for you.' I gave him my name and asked if it would be wise to go to a church on the Sunday. 'Let me advise you,' he replied. 'The church is being persecuted by the communist authorities and you must be very careful. Where are you staying?' 'The Ben Thanh Hotel,' I told him. He got out a piece of paper and drew a small map. 'I know the Ben Thanh well. It's near the large protestant church in Saigon. You'll have a so-called tourist guide allotted to take care of you. He's a member of the secret police. Ask him if he will accompany you to the church. If he agrees, it is safe for you to go, but don't talk to the pastor or anyone else because that could make trouble for them and for you. If he won't go, take my advice and don't go alone.'

On arrival in Saigon I was presented with three forms to complete. They all carried captions of 'Freedom and Happiness in Communist Vietnam'. Having completed the Immigration formalities, I boarded a crowded mini bus to go to the hotel. The city was noisy and the roads were full of bicycles and motor bikes, all keeping up an incessant hooting of bells and horns. We passed buildings covered with barbed wire with roofs of corrugated iron sheets rusted with age. As we approached the centre I could see that the city had once had a French elegance about it, though everything now looked worn out and in need of repair. I checked in at the hotel and was shown to my room. It was simply furnished, clean and comfortable. Then I asked the receptionist to make the necessary arrangements for Hai to come to the hotel. She did so and told me he was coming on the Sunday morning. That answered my question about going to church, I would not be free to go. In my luggage was a large sum of American dollars for Hai from Minh and Anh.

In the evening, as I was not allowed to leave the hotel unaccompanied, I went to the roof garden. A group of Westerners sat at another table and one of them called me over. 'What are you doing here?' they asked. 'Is it so unusual for an English person to be in Vietnam?' I responded, then enquired what they were doing. 'Don't you know? they answered. 'There's a journalists conference on in the hotel and we're all journalists. The Vietnamese are trying to open the country for tourism and they want to give us a good impression.'

Two older men introduced themselves, they were both American. One worked for *Reuters International* and the other was with *The Washington Post*. 'We're really interested in what could bring you here on your own,' they said. I told them about my work with the British Refugee Council and Southeast Asian Outreach and how, through Minh and Anh, I was now in Vietnam to meet their eldest brother, explaining that he had been in prison ten years as a former Naval Commander. 'Gee, honey,' one of them said, 'Don't you know that's a dangerous mission? You could be in trouble with the secret police.' 'I've obtained the full permission of the authorities and my application went through the Hanoi Embassy. I can't see how that could get me into trouble,' I assured him. The men looked serious. 'The Vietnamese are very suspicious and they don't trust Westerners,' one of them said. 'What time is your friend coming here?' he asked. I told them that Hai was due at 11.00am the following day. They said they would sit at a nearby table just in case there were problems. I thanked the men, then went to my room to read my Bible and have a time of prayer.

Before going to bed, I stood on my small balcony for some time, looking down on that great sprawling city with its noisy traffic and its thousands of people ruled by a Communist government. I had been told Christians were persecuted in Saigon, and that some were in prison for their faith. What did I know about following the Lord in such hard circumstances? Although I knew no Vietnamese Christians I prayed for God's people here in that city and especially for Hai, that he would be led to Christ.

Sunday morning was just as noisy as any other day in Saigon. As the tourist guide allotted to take care of me was not in reception when I looked around, I slipped out for a walk before Hai arrived. There was a large Roman Catholic cathedral nearby and the pavements were crowded with people doing their shopping. I marvelled at the skill of a woman who walked with two laden panniers held together by a yoke across the shoulders. In one pannier were live chicks and the other held ducklings. Vegetables and fruit were transported in the same manner. A shoe repairer sat on the pavement plying his trade.

Tired and thirsty in the heat, I soon made my way back to the hotel where I sat on the roof gardens sipping a fruit juice and watching the busy traffic below. Hai arrived promptly and, as he did, I observed two armed and uniformed young men take their place at the door leading back into the hotel from the roof garden. I opened the large parcels Hai brought for me and found they contained pictures done in the distinctive black laquerware with inlaid mother of pearl that is characteristic of Vietnamese art. I thanked him very much for this kindness, knowing how difficult his circumstances were. His English was perfect and he looked just like an older version of Minh. The photographs I gave him of Minh and Anh had their gift of dollars tucked in between them. We had to be very careful as we were being watched.

The police were quite a distance away and

certainly not within earshot because of the traffic noise. 'Tell me what has happened since you were released from prison,' I said.

'Mrs. Brenda,' Hai replied, 'I can't thank you enough for coming. I still don't know why I was released from prison so early. Most of my contemporaries are still in jail and I did not expect to be freed so soon. When I came back to Saigon I found my home had been confiscated. As it's now being used as an infant school I have a room with my elderly parents. Life here is very difficult. With my record of serving the Americans I cannot get employment. And I refuse to be a communist. Look what communism is doing to my country! Everyone is poor and there is no progress. I travelled extensively when I was in the Navy and visited many European ports. We are now years behind all these countries,' he concluded sadly.

'What are you doing for a living?' I asked.

'Because my English is good they have given me the task of teaching English to these secret police, the young ones there who are watching us!' he said.

'Minh and Anh are applying for you to go to America. What do you feel about that?' I asked.

'I want to see my wife and children again. They won't know me I suppose. It's so long since I saw them. My daughter was three years old when she left Vietnam. She is now fifteen. Have you seen them?' he enquired.

'Yes,' I told him. 'My husband and I went to the States a year ago and visited Minh and Anh. I also met your family. Your four children have grown into good looking people, but sadly I did not get on well with your wife.'

He looked at me with tears in his eyes. 'I never hear from her and I have a feeling she has found someone else,' he admitted.

'She's now divorced, Hai,' I told him gently, knowing the pain it would cause him. Looking away across the rusty roof tops of this crowded city, Hai tried to control himself.

It was with great dignity he spoke again after a short silence. 'I might have known. Twelve years is a long time. But I still kept hoping she would remember me. Do my children want to see me?'

'Yes, Hai,' I assured him, 'they do. I had a talk with all of them and they send their love to you. Your daughter said she is looking forward to getting to know you.'

'Communism is terrible,' he told me. 'It has wrecked my family, ruined my life and my country. I will never get out of Vietnam because they refuse exit permits to people like me. I have no home now and no future.' Hai spoke with great sadness but no bitterness.

'There is hope even in these black circumstances. Somewhere there is a God who cares about you,' I said, feeling quite inadequate for this situation.

'I'm a Buddhist,' Hai replied. 'But this has not helped me. Tell me, who is this God who cares?'

We sat for an hour as I tried to tell him the simple gospel message. He listened intently then replied, 'I do not understand it all but I can see this God is very real to you.'

'He is the only hope we have in these circumstances,' I explained. 'And I know he can help you as he has helped me.' Passing him a Gideon New Testament under the table, I said, 'Read this, it will help you to understand.'

Hai then tape recorded messages for his family and I took some photos of him. 'Would you like to have lunch with me in the hotel?' I asked, placing the camera on the table. Hai accepted my invitation.

As I rose from the table a heavy hand clapped me on the shoulder. 'Come this way,' barked one of the armed policemen. The other one snatched my camera and recorder.

'Hand those back at once!' I demanded. 'You have no right to take my belongings! I asked permission at the Vietnamese Embassy in London and they were all declared on my customs form. Where are you taking me? I have done nothing to violate the laws of your country!' I spoke angrily as these hardened young men seemed so brash. 'You'll come with us,' one of them said firmly.

I saw the two Americans were watching carefully. 'Get your camera out and write an article for newspapers worldwide that this is Freedom and Happiness in Communist Vietnam!' I shouted to them in my alarm.

The policeman took his hands off my shoulder and, looking at the reporters, he asked, 'Are you going to do as she said?'

'Yes,' they both replied. 'This should help folk at home to come here for a tour!' Both Americans laughed at the joke.

The policeman handed back my camera and recorder. Thanking them for their 'courtesy', I told them that Hai was having lunch with me in the dining room. They accompanied us and gave some instructions to the waiter. He moved a table away from the rest and we ate lunch in quiet isolation.

'Will you be all right when I've left Vietnam after all this?' I asked Hai.

'Yes,' he replied. 'There's nothing more they can take from me.'

After we had eaten, the police escorted Hai to reception and reminded me that I was not allowed to leave the hotel without their permission. As Hai walked through the entrance door, he brushed away tears and waved good bye.

Alone in my room, I prayed that God would

speak to Hai in all his need, and come into his sad circumstances in a way I could not even imagine. And, feeling rather shaken, I asked God for protection from danger during the following two days before I returned to Bangkok. There was a small swimming pool on the roof garden. I had a swim and relaxed in the blazing heat of the tropical sun to ease away my tension.

In the morning two armed police were waiting for me in reception. 'Where are you going today?' they asked.

'I don't know,' I replied, smiling. 'But I thought I might join a small group on a tour.'

'You are not allowed to go with the others,' one of them said. 'We will take you on a tour. Where would you like to go?' Knowing it was a long way away, and that it would take the whole day, I told them I would like to see the Mekong River. 'Come with us,' they said in a much more friendly manner. There was a chauffeur driven Mercedes Benz waiting for us outside the hotel. I got in and we drove out of the city into the countryside.

The scenery on the road to the Mekong was flat and mostly rice paddy fields. Buffalos pulled carts along the road. When we reached a market I got out for a walk. There were stalls of vegetables, strange looking fish and some bad smelling meat. I trod gingerly as the standard of hygiene was quite appalling. We were walking in inches of foul smelling mud. I felt sorry for the live ducks and chickens squawking in their small tight cages. People bought two or three ducks at a time, putting them into their bicycle baskets and securing their legs with a piece of string. One man had a very large basket on the back of his bicycle with a pig inside it!

When we arrived at the Mekong River there was a dilapidated landing stage with an old wooden boat tied alongside. We boarded the craft and chugged downstream towards an area that had wide fishing nets stretching halfway across the river. On either side were dense tropical plants and trees with brilliantly coloured kingfishers darting in and out of the foliage. Passing the remains of a partially sunk warship, I was fascinated to see that some families had converted it into their home. Washing was laid out on one deck, children played on another, and some young people fished from the rear. We saw small village settlements of rice straw houses built on stilts. When the tide was low these houses were in deep mud and I watched children playing nearby, waist high in the stuff!

The boat stopped at a landing stage. We scrambled out and walked through a forest path to a fruit farm. My escorts, who had become quite friendly, showed me the various tropical fruits that grew there. I did not know the English names and was therefore none the wiser, as I had never seen them before. Stopping at a small wooden house, we had a cup of tea and a rest before returning to the boat. As the roads were poor and full of potholes the journey back took nearly two hours.

The next day I was glad to return to Bangkok, as the abject poverty of Vietnam depressed me, even though the people are resourceful and cheerful. I was pleased to have met Hai. My films and recordings were safe! And, as I had brought Hai's papers with me for the application to go to America, I was able to lodge them at the Orderly Departure Programme in Bangkok. I had one more day in Thailand before my flight to Burma.

The Vice-Consul from the British Embassy in Rangoon met me at the airport and took me to the hotel. He told me that Grace was extremely ill and advised me to take great care on my visits as government security had tightened and it was likely that my movements would be watched. Arranging for an Embassy official to go ahead of me to Grace's house, the Vice-Consul told me that his son would collect me later and take me back to the hotel.

It was dark when I entered Grace's home. There was a power cut and it was dimly lit with candles. Climbing up a wooden ladder to the floor above, I found my friend lying on a thin mattress on the floor. I had forgotten how poor her home was, quite lacking in any comfort.

Grace looked very ill. She told me that she had cancer and had been ill since 1988 when she had witnessed unforgettable scenes. On 8th August of that year there was an uprising, mainly of students, against the military regime when the League for Democracy won the General Election and the junta refused to hand over power.

The army had opened fire on the demonstrators and thousands were killed, she explained. The street in front of her home was strewn with bodies and awash with blood. 'I never believed I would live to see such carnage,' she said, her voice shaking. 'I even saw young mothers with babies mown down. At the end of the day bodies were stacked eight high against the walls. Soldiers drove trucks in the evening and collected the bodies like refuse and took them to an incinerator. We are safe here to speak freely,' Grace assured me, 'but outside no one dares to say a word.'

My friend shared appalling things with me. 'Despite my illness I still fast and pray every Friday, first for my family and then for my country,' she concluded. 'Two other women from the church join me in prayer.' I told Grace that Christians from the west could learn a great deal from her level of commitment. I felt it was a great honour to be in this poor little room with such a woman of prayer. We had not known one another for long, but there was a very deep bond of affection between us. Later, as I checked into my room at the Inya Lake Hotel, I felt glad that I had made this visit. Conditions in the hotel hadn't changed and my old friends the cockroaches were there to greet me!

Ronnie, the Burmese elder from the church at which Stephen had become a Christian, collected me the following morning to take me to the service. I received a very warm welcome, and after the service was inundated with enquiries about Stephen. There was a beauty about the service that I had not experienced elsewhere, such joy in the singing and a great reverence in worship. I was introduced to many of the people Ronnie cared for. Eleven widows and seven orphans were supported by this church. In addition he regularly took a number of disabled patients out for the day from a hospital for the chronically sick. Knowing the poverty of these people I asked him how he managed to do so much. 'Things are very difficult for us now,' he explained. 'Inflation is so high that many can barely afford to eat. Yet we are compelled to praise our God, for we are daily experiencing the reality of "Abiding in the Shadow of the Almighty". He cares about each detail of our lives and never fails to richly supply all our needs.' What a stark contrast to the begging bowls of the Buddhist monks!

That evening Ronnie and his wife joined me

for dinner at the hotel. I noted the respect with which the waiter served him, and that the meal he was given was of far better standard than usual. Ronnie provided the explanation. 'The waiter's mother died a few months ago and I went to visit him. He lives in a small wooden shack and has no possessions. I spoke to him about Christ being the Resurrection and the Life and he appreciated my care. He asked me to bury his mother and we had a simple service. He's been coming to the church ever since when he has time off. Spreading the gospel here is not allowed but we use every opportunity that is presented to us privately. We take great care to obey the government's laws because the Bible instructs us to do so in Romans 13:1-6.'

The dismal decor of the dining room seemed lighter in the company of these dedicated Christians. We laughed and talked together until just before the curfew. This was imposed by the military junta after the demonstrations, and it was still in force. I called to see Grace the next day before my flight to Bangkok. As I flew out of that fascinating city, I had much to reflect on concerning the lives of my Burmese Christian friends.

CHAPTER ELEVEN

NEW DIRECTION

'Only one life, 'twil soon be past, only what's done for Christ will last,' wrote Stephen Olford. These words came home with renewed power as I opened my post one beautiful spring morning in 1989 and read a very brief note from my youngest brother. It informed me that our father had died and was buried. When I tried to telephone my stepmother, she hung up when she heard my voice. I reflected over the years when he had been a wonderful father, remembering the happiness of our home and the strong Christian teaching that had been an invaluable part of my upbringing. That stood in such stark contrast to the extreme separatist doctrine which barred me from even attending my father's funeral. My eldest brother received a similar notification.

United in our grief, we went together to the cemetery in Guildford where Philip and my mother had been laid to rest. Daffodils nodded in the gentle breeze and the trees were in full blossom. 'I am the Resurrection and the Life,' the Lord said to me through his beautiful creation. We laid a simple bunch of flowers on the grave and stood there in tears as we thought of the father we had not seen for nearly twenty years.

The following week a telegram arrived from Burma to say that Grace had died. My memories of her courage and dedication to Christ have remained with me to this day. The beautiful jewel box with her hand written note inside, 'With all my love, and may God be with you until we meet again,' now had a new meaning. We shall meet again in the heavenly city, the new Jerusalem, where 'there will be no more death or mourning or crying or pain, for the old order of things has passed away' (Revelation 21:4).

As my work in caring for the refugees was now winding down, I prayed that God would direct me into new ways in which I could help with the needs in their home countries. About that time I was approached by the specialist who had looked after my health for many years, and asked by him to help organise an appeal he was launching for a new unit at our local hospital. I felt I owed this doctor a great deal. He was the only person in whom I had confided the troubles of my background. Although I had never been involved in fund raising, I took it on. It was an entirely new venture. The work was demanding but very interesting, and our efforts were varied and successful. We even organised gala concerts at Eton College! And I was able to use my previous professional experience when giving fund-raising talks in schools.

I spent nearly three years helping with the appeal and was honoured to be present at the unit's official opening by Princess Alexandra. However I was not at peace with my conscience, and words from the epistle of James frequently came to mind, 'Friendship of the world is enmity with God' (James 4:4, AV). When we reached the final target I decided to resign and use my newly gained experience in Christian work.

I loved being back in the peaceful surroundings of the wooded countryside, yet I was not at peace with my own conscience. One warm Sunday evening in 1989, we decided to go to All Souls Church, Langham Place in London, to attend a special series of meetings that took place in the month of August. The final sermon was on the Cross and the need never to forget the cost of our redemption. There is a beautiful oil painting in this church which portrays Christ being presented to the crowd before his crucifixion. Our Lord is depicted wearing the purple robe and the crown of thorns. I gazed at this painting as I sang the closing hymn.

When I survey the wondrous cross,
On which the Prince of Glory died
My richest gain I count but loss,
And pour contempt on all my pride.

Were the whole realm of nature mine,
That were an offering far too small,
Love so amazing, so divine
Demands my soul, my life, my all.

(Isaac Watts)

That evening I thanked the Lord for giving me the hospital work to do and asked him to direct me into similar avenues in Christian mission, resolving to live my life only in the service of my Master. He nowhere offers us an easy life, but he does promise to be with us in every circumstance. To live in his company is the greatest ideal for Christian service.

Following that experience I had talks with World Vision, one of the leading aid agencies. It works in nearly a hundred countries, helping over sixty million people in their struggle against poverty, hunger and injustice. I decided to use my hospital experience to help raise funds for their projects in Southeast Asia. In the autumn I made plans to see some of the many aid programmes World Vision were running in Thailand, and to visit a children's hospital they had funded and built in Phnom Penh, Cambodia's capital city. As I had kept in touch with Ronnie's church in Rangoon and was aware of his congregational needs, I also arranged to have a few days there and to take some support for the widows and orphans he cared for.

We had a happy Christmas before my Far East tour. Our daughters, son-in-law and our lovely little granddaughter came one day and our extended family the following. Stephen and Ponnie were there. And we were especially glad that Christopher came and brought his wife. Tien, who had graduated from university and obtained a job as social services coordinator with a London council, came with his wife and two daughters. We were very proud of Tien's achievements. Events have now gone full circle as he has since been appointed to the advisory committee of British Refugee Council, the very organisation that put me in touch with him when he first came to England as a refugee.

It was a cold January day in 1990 when I left Heathrow for Bangkok. Thida, who was very excited at the prospect of me visiting her country for the first time, asked me to bring her back lots of photos. She gave me details of where she had lived in Phnom Penh so that I could photograph the house for her. 'Would you like to go back?' I asked her. Thida's face clouded over with fear. 'No, not while the Khmer Rouge are still there,' she replied. 'I would never live with any feelings of safety in my country.' And, looking at her little daughter she added, 'I have to speak in Cambodian to her or she will never know she is Cambodian.' Seeing Thida's expression made me realise how difficult it is to be an alien in a foreign land and how much we take our freedom for granted.

My plane landed at Bangkok and I went to the airport hotel once again. It takes a few days to become acclimatised to the steamy heat of this busy city. After a short rest I walked to a nearby shopping area to get some exercise. I had forgotten about the mixture of smells from the street vendors' stalls with their variety of cooked foods, the mangy dogs and scruffy cats that lay asleep in the heat of the sun on the crowded pavements and the tinkling of bells from a gaudily painted Buddhist temple.

The following morning I awoke early, as I was going to the head office of World Vision Foundation of Thailand and, knowing the traffic problems, I called a taxi immediately after breakfast. On arrival I met a number of staff members and arrangements were made to take me to see several projects in and around Bangkok. As I travelled by mini bus with one of the Thai workers I was very interested to hear how he had become a Christian in this staunchly Buddhist country. He first heard the gospel message on a radio programme broadcast by the Far East Broadcasting Company. I told him I was later going to revisit Rangoon, Burma and that my friend there was Director of FEBC.

As we moved slowly through the crowded traffic Don, the Thai worker, explained that we were going to the Bangkok slums. I had read about this project before I left England, but nothing could have prepared me for the conditions of these slum dwellers. They defied description. There were hundreds of poorly erected wooden shacks built over foul smelling green swamps filled with rubbish and teeming with flies. I saw one little boy drinking water from a stagnant water butt. As we walked along the planks over these swamplands, Don explained that World Vision was seeking to assist these people through a programme of health care, hygiene, education and training in handicrafts, in the hope that they would then be able to help themselves in building a better life.

World Vision worked alongside local people trained in medical care and hygiene, and there was a clinic to which children could be taken for immunisation. Mothers were encouraged to send their children to primary school where they would learn skills to equip them for a better future. I watched some women who were already benefiting from this new project, as they embroidered jumpers to earn enough money to feed their families. On our walk we passed many scruffy dogs that were covered in fleas and mangy cats with fierce looking faces. No doubt they had learned to survive the hard way in this deprived area! Don told me that plans were being made to improve the lot of these slum dwellers, and I thought of the important part Christians play in helping such poverty-stricken areas.

We reboarded the mini bus and drove several miles out of the city to an area the tourist certainly never sees. I thought that Bangkok's slums must be the worst place in the world to live, but as we approached Garbage City, my eyes could hardly take in what they were seeing. For miles and miles in every direction stretched mountains of filthy stinking refuse. The whole area was a dirty grey colour and smoke from burning refuse filled the air. I could not believe that anyone lived there but, as we travelled along the filthy roads, I saw the tin huts which served as homes. Don pointed out people scavenging among the refuse for pieces of white plastic which they sold to make a living. A refuse lorry passed on the other side of the road. It stopped to pick up a small boy who was waiting by the roadside in the stench and heat. As I watched, he climbed up the back of the lorry and sat on top of the refuse!

On the edge of this dreadful place sat a pleasing building which Don explained was a daycare centre run by World Vision. Walking around this well-appointed school, we watched small children playing with toys in a light airy room. Two hundred children are taken to the centre each day to be fed, clothed and receive primary school education. The Thai lady in charge was a lovely bright character, such a contrast to all around that was dark and depressing. She showed me the school books with World Vision's name on their backs. What an example of practical Christian care in action, setting these children up to face a brighter future.

In the afternoon we returned to the city and visited Emergency Home where World Vision works alongside the Thai government to help the helpless, give a temporary home to the homeless and destitute, and assist girls who have been forced into prostitution to begin to build new lives. As we were shown round the well maintained home, the friendly matron, in excellent English, introduced me to the staff and outlined the problems of some of the people they were helping.

Among those we met were two young mothers with babies whose husbands had been killed in road accidents, and a small boy, thought to be Bengali, who had been found in the streets and brought in for care. No-one could speak his language. There was a sad, hopeless looking thirteen year old girl whose father had sold her into prostitution to pay his gambling debts. She was so terrified in the brothel that she climbed out of the window and fell to the ground injuring herself badly. The matron told me that girls from country areas had never heard of VD let alone AIDS. As part of the rescue programme, the matron ran a class in which she taught the girls the dangers of drug abuse. After providing girls with teaching, support and medical care, they were trained for jobs such as hairdressing. On my visit I saw a blind old lady sitting on the floor. She had been dumped in the city centre by callous relatives who no longer wished to care for her. Before leaving the home I was shown a variety of handicrafts the residents had made, and which were being sold to raise funds.

It was a long day. And in it I saw some of the lowest and most desperate of human situations, into which World Vision was bringing new hope for a better future.

CHAPTER TWELVE

CAMBODIA

I was disappointed when I learned from my travel agent that my flight to Cambodia was scheduled to leave Saigon on the Sunday morning, as I had written to Hai telling him that I proposed to see him that weekend. Because the ordinary people of Vietnam do not have telephones it is difficult to make contact quickly. I was going to Vietnam with a small group of American tourists and we were all flying on to Cambodia for three or four days. Tour operators can never guarantee that their bookings operate as scheduled.

We landed in Saigon and drove to the hotel. When they saw the conditions, the Americans expressed their dissatisfaction loudly and finally most of them accepted accommodation elsewhere, leaving only three of the original group with me. As I watched the receptionist handling these difficult people, I particularly noticed one tall young Vietnamese man. There was something about him that I liked.

'Are you checking in here?' he asked me, as I was the last member of the group.

'Yes,' I replied. 'This hotel looks nice, in fact better than the Ben Thanh which I visited two years ago.'

'Are you on the tour?' he enquired politely.

As the other receptionists had left the desk, I felt I could trust this man. 'I'm supposed to be on the tour, but I've seen most of Saigon on a previous visit and I have a friend here that I wish to see.' I showed him Hai's name and address.

He looked very interested and asked, 'How do you know anyone here when you come from England?'

'I have three young Vietnamese people as part of my extended family,' I explained, 'and my friend is the eldest brother of one of them. I need to get a message to him, as he does not know which hotel I am in. Because my flight to Phnom Penh leaves very early Sunday morning I really need to see him as soon as possible.'

'I'll send someone to his address straight away,' he promised, smiling.

Feeling I could confide in him I said, 'My friend has had ten years in prison and two years in a re-education camp. He was a commander in the Navy.'

Looking round carefully, he then added quietly, 'My father is the same, he was a Colonel in the Army. I will help you as much as I can.' Showing me to my room, he said he would be back as soon as the message had been taken.

I had a very pleasant dinner with two of the tour group. One was an American doctor who was very interested in seeing Vietnamese culture.

The other man, who spoke with a European accent, told me he taught in the University of California and that he had a deep interest in the politics of these communist countries. I explained to them that I was not going on the tour in Cambodia but was visiting a children's hospital run by World Vision. They both knew about World Vision's work and spoke very highly of their aid programmes.

Soon after I went to my room, my young receptionist knocked on the door. 'I went to see Hai myself,' he told me. 'He was so pleased to know that you are here and asked if he could accompany me back to the hotel. He's waiting in the reception to see you.' I was delighted.

'How kind of you,' I said. 'By the way I am a Christian,' I explained, 'and that is why I help your people.'

'Me too,' the young man told me, his face lighting up with pleasure. He put his hand in his pocket. 'Here's my Bible,' he said, pulling out a well worn copy. 'I know a Christian taxi driver who will help you when you need to go out.'

Hai greeted me in reception. 'Mrs. Brenda, it's so good to see you again,' he smiled. 'So much has happened since your last visit. I hardly know where to start. I've got a letter for you to read.'

Puzzled that he should write me a letter, I opened the envelope and read it. It was an invitation to attend a church on the Sunday and conveyed Christian greetings to me from the pastor. 'This is a great surprise, Hai. Who is this pastor?' I asked. 'I've never been to a church service in Vietnam.'

'He's the man who led me to Christ. I'm now a Christian. Remember you told me about your faith?' he asked. 'When I left the hotel after your last visit I was in the depths of despair because I could see no future. I walked all the way home. It is about nine miles from here. When I reached my road I was exhausted and depressed. A man stopped me on the corner. He said, "You look upset. Can I help you?" He took me to his house for a cup of tea and I told him my story. Then he began to speak to me about the same Christian God that you had told me about and invited me to his church the following Sunday and I have attended there ever since. It has given me a new life to know Jesus Christ.'

My friend looked at me with eyes brimming with tears. This time they were tears of happiness. 'You will come to our church, won't you?' he enquired.

'As things stand at the moment, I fly to Cambodia on Sunday morning, so it will not be possible. But can you join me for dinner tomorrow evening at this hotel?' I asked.

'I'll look forward to that,' Hai said. 'But it's late now, and I must go home.'

I went to bed happy that evening, delighting in this remarkable answer to prayer. How can anyone say there is no God when such things as this happen?

In the morning the receptionist told me that there was a Christian taxi driver outside if I wished to see the city. So, armed with my camera, I decided to enjoy the day sightseeing before my early flight to Cambodia. We went to Ho Chi Minh's residence where we saw tableaux of the various stages of his life. These were made of delicately carved wood and straw. It was sad that things of such beauty commemorated a man who had driven his country into poverty and fear. My taxi driver and I walked along the river and watched the ships in the docks, then he took me to the workshops where lovely pictures were made, pictures such as Hai had given me on my previous visit. The artists' working conditions were very bad. Their room was poorly lit, and puddles of mud lay on the floors. Despite the great skill needed to produce these pictures, the driver told me their monthly wage was about three US dollars.

I went back to the hotel for a light lunch and, while I was in the dining room, the receptionist came to see me.

'Mrs. Brenda, your travel arrangements have been changed. There is no plane available for tomorrow's flight to Phnom Penh. They're now making arrangements for a flight early Monday morning.'

'That's good news!' I replied happily. 'I shall be able to go to church.'

Looking around carefully, he said quietly, 'I can arrange for you to come to my church. There are huge numbers. We haven't got enough seats. People listen outside under the windows.'

'Thank you very much,' I replied warmly. 'But Hai is now a Christian and I have an invitation to attend his church.'

The young man smiled happily. 'What time is the service?' he asked. 'I'll arrange for the Christian taxi driver to take you.'

I told him the time and the arrangements fell simply into place. That afternoon I visited the zoo, where I met a group of sweet little children obviously there on a special outing. They were all so beautifully dressed. The resourcefulness of these very poor people amazed me.

Hai joined me for dinner at the hotel in the evening. After we had ordered the meal he said, 'I have more news for you. When I became a Christian I asked God to help me leave Vietnam. You took my papers to the Orderly Departure Programme in Bangkok. This week I had a letter from the authorities telling me that my exit visa is to be granted in two months time. God has done this and answered my prayers.' I was thrilled, and told Hai that I would telephone him when he arrived in America to start a new life there. The rest of the evening passed very quickly as we talked about Minh and Anh and their flat in Texas.

When I woke very early Sunday morning I felt a great sense of gratitude to God who was allowing me the privilege of attending a Christian gathering in Vietnam. After travelling about nine miles out of the city, to a very poor area with pot-holed roads and shabby dwellings, we reached the church. Hai was waiting at the door to greet me and we went together into the newly whitewashed building. It was a simple brick structure with an apparently disused building alongside that looked like a school. I sat down on a well worn bamboo bench, happy in the company of my fellow Christians. Hai translated the service, which was very long but full of life and joy. The singing was accompanied by an electric guitar and it was quite beautiful. At the end of the service I was invited on to the platform and handed the microphone. Controlling deep emotions, I thanked the people for their invitation and gave greetings to them all. I also thanked them for the help they had given Hai. Having promised to pray for them each day, I asked them to pray for their brothers and sisters in Burma and Cambodia, telling them that I was to visit these countries later.

The pastor told me that the congregation had

a gospel outreach to the Cambodian borders and many people there had become Christians. Taking me outside he said, 'This church was confiscated by the government for fourteen years and during that time we were not allowed to meet together. We met secretly in one another's homes. There are now over one hundred house fellowships. As we are only allowed a certain number in the church we take it in turns to meet here. We are watched by government officers and they don't like to see our numbers increase as they think we will believe in our God more than in them! Please ask Christians in England to pray for our safety. That school near the church used to be run by us and we had a small medical clinic there too. Our people are so poor they can't pay for a doctor.' He went on, 'When we built the church with the school and clinic we were helped by a Christian organisation called World Vision. Have you heard of it in England?' I told him that it was their hospital that I was visiting in Cambodia!

On Monday morning we were driven to the airport for the flight to Cambodia. A two hour delay followed and I passed the time happily reading a book. When our flight was ready we walked across the tarmac to a small ancient-looking plane. As we entered we put our bags on the floor of the rear section. I thought Burma Airways was bad, but this was worse! When we finally took off the plane filled with steam from the outdated oxygen supply. Although it was a bumpy landing at Pochentong Airport I was glad to have arrived. The short bus journey to the hotel was interesting, as it took us along pleasant roads lined with palm trees and between fields in which buffalo grazed. When we approached the city I was quite taken aback by the beauty of the place, probably because the television documentaries I had seen about Cambodia had shown the worst parts.

The Director of World Vision of Cambodia was waiting at my hotel to greet me. As my flight was so late he thought it best that I see the hospital the next day. On the flight from Saigon I had sat next to a journalist from the *Sunday Telegraph* and he asked me to get him permission to go to the hospital. The Director agreed. Arrangements having been made, I set off in a taxi with the doctor from America, the journalist and the lecturer from California University, to view the city. The taxi driver told us he was taking us to Toul Sleng, one of the centres at which Pol Pot had tortured his own people. We drove along wide tree-lined boulevards. The houses were built in French style with shutters to keep out the heat. There was a large number of trees and green open spaces where cyclo drivers waited for customers. Cyclos are tricycles with a seat on the front to take passengers. Roadside vendors sold coconut milk and Coca Cola.

The centre we were taken to had barbed wire over the windows, although it had clearly once been a school. Our guide took us through the torture chambers which had been left as they were found by the Vietnamese soldiers when they ousted the Khmer Rouge. There were spine chilling photos on the walls of blackened corpses lying on the blood stained floors, iron bedsteads with metal shackles which had held victims while instruments of torture, that went back to the dark ages, were applied. We walked in silence through these grotesque rooms before coming out again into bright sunlight, only to be confronted with gallows on which people had been hung upside down and dropped into tubs of cold water to drown. Our tour finished in a small hall, on the walls of which were photos of members of the Khmer Rouge throwing babies into the air and shooting at them with their rifles.

'This is worse than Aushwitz. So terrible is this people's suffering. It's worse than the Nazi concentration camps,' said the lecturer from California University. He spoke with a heavy European accent and tears rolled down his cheeks. I wondered about his history, but asked no question. None of us felt like speaking as the taxi driver took us out of the city towards the 'Killing Fields'.

There was a unique charm about the

countryside, with its small settlements of straw houses set among coconut palms and breadfruit trees. We got out of the car and stood in the shade of some trees and the driver went ahead to a gate covered in barbed wire. Walking silently through the peaceful meadow we came to a huge monument. Behind its glazed front was shelf after shelf of skulls, arranged by order of age. All around were mass graves where thousands of people were buried after they had been tortured at Toul Sleng. Even nature seemed silent. I could not hear a bird singing.

A missionary once told me that if you want to serve a country you have to weep over it, as Christ wept over Jerusalem. I didn't fully understand that until I stood face to face with what lay before me that day.

That experience, which could have thrown me into deep despair, was redeemed by God. He used it to motivate me. Such was my passion for the work World Vision was doing among the traumatised people of Cambodia, that over three thousand pounds was raised over the following three months of speaking engagements.

We ate as a group that evening, bound together by our shared experience. Afterwards I spoke with the lecturer, who was not feeling well. He told me he originated from Hungary and that, when he was thirteen years old, the Nazis overran his country and he was taken to Aushwitz. His family were Jews. Every relative apart from his mother died in the gas chambers. 'I eventually got political asylum in America after I had had several years in exile in the Gulag,' he explained. 'I am now a Professor in Eastern European History. It's so sad that people in the world never learn lessons from history and man's inhumanity to his fellow man goes on, especially in communist countries. They say there is no god, so they have no respect for man.'

Cockerels crowing woke me at the crack of dawn the next morning. I dressed and went outside. Standing on the banks of the Mekong River, I watched as the sun, a great golden ball of light, rose from the horizon. The dark sky mellowed to a soft pink and the rising sun threw a pathway of shimmering gold down the river, silhouetting the fishing nets left there to catch crabs. Sunrays lit up the brilliantly coloured bouganvillas in the hotel gardens. In that beauty and quietude it was not difficult to imagine the terror the people must have felt as bombs dropped on their peaceful city. Only a short distance down the river were the remains of a bridge that had been blown up.

In the fresh, clean air of the morning I walked out of the gardens and down the quiet road past a large hotel being built in the traditional Cambodian architecture that blended so well with the landscape. But my leisure was limited, as World Vision had arranged early transport to take me to the hospital. Tourists were having their breakfast on the benches and tables outside the hotel before leaving to visit Angkor Wat, an ancient Buddhist temple area renowned for its beauty. I checked my camera and recording equipment, as I was making audio-visual films for World Vision's work.

The hospital, a one storey building, sat in several acres of land part of which was a large children's playground. The Director of World Vision Cambodia introduced me to other visitors, among them a television crew and the Director of World Vision Germany, as well as the *Telegraph* reporter. The hospital's large reception area was crowded with mothers holding crying babies and young children. The Director told us that the staff frequently saw eleven hundred children a day, as this was the only children's hospital in the country! We were introduced to a tall Cambodian man who was the hospital director and professor in paediatrics. He was one of the few doctors who survived the infamous killings. When Pol Pot's reign of terror was over only twenty-five doctors were left in the country. When I visited the hospital, which is an internationally accepted training centre, it had ninety-two medical students. I met some of them and noted that a good proportion of those training to be doctors were women.

We visited wards where children were being treated for cholera, typhoid, tetanus and measles. Others had dengue fever, which can be fatal, meningitis and bronchial pneumonia. The most pathetic little children were those in the specialist ward for the treatment of malnutrition. Some hardly looked like children at all, and I was told that many of them would die because they were brought to the hospital too late.

As we walked into another ward, a couple brought in their very sick three-year-old daughter. Seeing the seriousness of her condition, two doctors quickly lifted the child to a table to examine her. To my surprise the father lay down on the floor and fell asleep, while the mother sat on a chair, speaking to the doctors through her tears. For half an hour the staff fought to save the child's life. Despite their best efforts the little girl died. A nurse told me the parents had travelled over one hundred miles to come to the hospital, spending the equivalent of a month's wages on bus fares. The little girl, who had septicaemia, had been taken to a Buddhist monk who gave her an injection of some unknown fluid. When that had not helped, they brought her to the hospital – but too late.

When her daughter died, the mother kicked her husband awake and shouted angrily at him. Seeing the dead child, he removed his krama (a red and white check type of turban), and wrapped the little body in it. One of the doctors gave the parents, from his own pocket, the money for their bus fare home. They left, taking their daughter's body with them to bury in their home village. The infrastructure of Cambodia was so wrecked by the years of war that their journey home could take them two or three days. The *Telegraph* reporter, who had a three-year-old son, was in tears as he wrote his notes.

On a visit to the pathology laboratory I noted that, while it was very well equipped, the methods being used for diagnostic tests were still those that I had learnt years before, methods that would now be considered very out of date in England. I commented on this to one of the doctors and he explained that this was deliberate, as the laboratory had frequent power cuts and could not rely on electricity.

We were taken to the outpatients clinic where they weighed the babies and immunised them against preventable illnesses. Observing a corridor with some patients lying on the floor, I asked if they had plans to extend the hospital. It was explained to me, that as they had a policy never to turn away a sick child, in the rainy season they were very overcrowded, but that World Vision felt that RINE centres (rehydration, immunisation, nutrition and education) were more urgently needed than a hospital extension. RINE centres in the rural areas aimed to prevent deaths such as we witnessed. World Vision regularly uses cartoon type programmes on Cambodian television to promote health awareness, family planning, hygiene and immunisation.

As it was early afternoon when I returned to the hotel, I took a short rest before walking through the gardens and along the road to where the cyclo riders waited. They were all keen to try out their English on me! Eventually I hired one to take me to the Royal Palace that had been King Sihanouk's residence. We stopped for a drink of coconut milk and I took some photographs. There were cows grazing on what had clearly been parkland at one time, and in the city centre pigs wandered across the road and chickens and cockerels were everywhere. Fascinated by this, I asked my driver if animals had always been in the city. He shook his head and said by way of explanation, 'Pol Pot's soldiers killed all the city people and stole their houses. Most of his men came from peasant areas and had no education at all.' 'Was anyone in your family killed?' I asked. 'Yes,' he replied. 'My father and two sisters. Everyone has had part of his family killed by Pol Pot.'

The Royal Palace was a magnificent building furnished lavishly with beautiful antique furniture, mostly in French style. The intricate woodcarvings and silver work set with rubies and sapphires made it a wonderful place to visit. Sihanouk's throne was quite spectacular. And the palace floor, on which I walked barefoot was made of silver! Outside were beautiful gardens with colourful flower beds. In the midst of the beauty I suddenly felt very tired and depressed. Turning my back on it all, I took a cyclo back to the hotel. I could not get out of my mind the awful picture of that little dying three-year-old. Thida's daughter was three, and I thought of her lovely home and of all the medical care she had in England. It was hard to believe that only twelve years ago her mother had been driven from her home in this city to work as a slave in the 'killing fields'.

We had our last Cambodian meal on a floating restaurant on the river before going to the airport. On arriving back in Bangkok I made arrangements to fly to the southern peninsula of Thailand that bordered on Malaysia, as World Vision had several projects they wanted me to see there. I boarded a small aeroplane at the domestic airport and flew to Nakhorn Si Thammarat, then took a taxi out of that rather uninteresting Thai town to another smaller one where World Vision had a field office. Two young Thai project workers and a girl called Supida accompanied me. As the village they were assisting was still quite a distance away, we began the journey by motor cycle and sidecar, the likes of which we don't have in England. In Cambodia they are commonly used to take pigs to market! I climbed aboard and hung on to the rails.

Having bumped along the uneven roads for some time, we then went along a few miles of grass track before reaching a wide river. We took a ferry across the river and proceeded further into the country via another grass track. This led to a narrow waterway where there were several dugout canoes tied to a landing stage. I climbed aboard one of the canoes and we travelled upstream for an hour and a half. Either side of the klong (canal) there were rough straw houses, many of them badly damaged and deserted looking. Supida told me that World Vision had assisted in this area the previous year after serious flooding. The whole area had been salienated and clean water supplies were laid on by World Vision.

Further upstream there was no sign of any human habitation. Along either side of the klong were deep banks of tropical vegetation with blue water hyacinths growing alongside pink and white lilies. Other canoes came towards us and then suddenly we came upon a small bridge spanning the waterway. A banner on it read, 'Welcome to Gong Hong village.' 'That banner is there for you,' Supida said. We stepped ashore and walked to the village. All the children there had sponsors in England. Everyone came out to greet us.

As part of our tour we were taken to the school in the centre of the village and Supida translated for the headmaster. The children, who were all neatly dressed in school uniforms, looked very happy and healthy. There was a small dental and medical clinic where the children were issued with toothbrushes and toothpaste. A banquet of local prawns and crabs was laid on for us. All the mothers and fathers came to watch us eat! Supida told me I was probably the first English woman that they had seen. We visited three other villages by the same mode of transport. At the last one there was a table of beautifully presented fresh fruits and a welcome cup of tea. It was a long interesting day and I slept well that night before flying back to Bangkok.

CHAPTER THIRTEEN

LIVING IN FEAR

I enjoyed a relaxing day at the airport hotel pool before flying out to Rangoon. As the Vice Consul had asked me to take him some hair cream and English chocolate, I packed them in my overnight bag for the flight to Burma. The Thai Airways flight was delayed an hour and a half. I wondered why, as these flights are usually very punctual. Eventually a larger aircraft was laid on for the flight and, a quarter of an hour before the new departure time, ten or twelve armed Thai police came into the room. They were joined by government officials, then about one hundred Burmese young people, looking bedraggled and frightened, were escorted on to the plane.

I sat on the plane next to an attaché from the Indian Embassy in Rangoon. He told me that the young people were students who had survived the protests for democracy, then fled for safety to the Thai border. But they sought refuge at the border only to be arrested by Thai customs officers and taken to a prison camp before being forcibly returned to Rangoon. 'What will happen to them now?' I asked. 'No one knows,' he replied. 'The military junta is a wicked regime. It is just a group of bandits who have no idea how to rule. Everyone hates the government. It is so incompetent, I cannot believe it will last. But anyone who opposes it either disappears or is put in prison. I doubt if any of these students will ever reach home again.'

On landing at Mingaladon Airport we had to wait while the students were marched into the airport. By the time we were allowed into the hot and stuffy lounge the students had gone. When I had retrieved my overnight bag from the stern and unfriendly customs officers, I looked around for Mr. V, the Vice Consul, who had promised to be there. He had arranged to meet me as a friend, not in any official capacity. He was now semi-retired though still working at the Embassy. A smartly dressed Burmese girl called my name and asked me to accompany her. I explained that Mr. V was somewhere in the building. 'No, he isn't,' she replied curtly. 'You are to be taken to the hotel by me.' As my protests fell on deaf ears, I got into the waiting car.

'I need to know the names and addresses of people you are visiting,' my companion told me as we drove along. 'Why do you need this?' I asked, immediately on guard. 'Government regulations,' she replied. I did not answer. She then looked at the palm of her hand on which something was written in ink. 'You will be meeting Grace Aung Pe: U. Ba Hlang,' the young woman said. I was taken aback that she had a list of my friends. 'Some of those are dead. Your records are not up to date,' I told her. 'As Mr. V normally meets me and I register at the British Embassy, perhaps you would be kind enough to take me there.' 'You don't need to go,' she insisted. 'I'm taking you to the hotel.' 'That's fine,' I said, 'but perhaps you will wait and take me to the Embassy. I only have an overnight bag.' She did not reply and we drove the remaining distance in silence.

Having checked in, I asked my guide to take me to the Embassy. As we drove along the familiar roads I noticed that the tree trunks had been whitewashed and dilapidated buildings were getting a coat of paint too. Commenting on this my guide said, 'This new government is really good. They are really improving everything for the people. I will wait here in the car while you go into the Embassy,' she added, as we had arrived there. I recognised the Burmese man who was in the doorway. 'Where's Mr. V?' I asked. 'He was supposed to be meeting me at the airport.' 'He's at the airport to meet you,' he replied. Then, looking out at the parked car, he asked, 'Where did you get that car from? Your guide's a government spy. Go and pay them off with a few American dollars.' The driver and guide accepted the dollars and drove off. 'You can't trust anyone now,' he said. 'Come inside.' When I asked to use the phone and he said, 'Go ahead, but please be careful. Our lines are bugged, so mind what you say.' I spoke briefly to Ronnie and he arranged to collect me from the hotel early on Sunday morning. The official called a taxi to take me to Mr. V's house.

We travelled into an area of Rangoon I had not seen before. The houses were poorly erected wooden structures and our car bumped up and down so badly on the pot-holed road that I was relieved to get out. Mr. V's home was situated at the end of a road in quite a large compound. His wife greeted me and told me that her husband had gone to the airport. She advised me to take great caution on this brief visit as everyone lived in fear of the government. Later, when her husband arrived, he expressed surprise at seeing me in his house. I explained what had happened before he drove me to my hotel.

It was too late for dinner and, as I had eaten a meal on the plane, I decided to have an early night. When I found that the lock on my door did not function I went to reception to ask for it to be attended to, but was told it could not be done until morning. Feeling uneasy, I unpacked my bag and put my clothes in the dusty cupboard. The air conditioner was working but it was so noisy it was like having a car engine running in the room! As I could not read in the dimly lit room, I tried to sleep. Having dozed off, I woke with a start as the door opened and a figure came toward me. 'Get out of my room!' I shouted. I reached the corridor in time to see a scruffily dressed Burmese man running towards the lift. I looked at my watch. It was 1.30am. Putting my bag in front of the door, I lay down again and tried to sleep. After a fitful night, I rose early and dressed for a walk.

There was no one about as I wandered around the reception area and looked at the display of Burmese jewels and pearls. Some of the most beautiful rubies, sapphires and pearls come from this country, and it used to export quantities of oil, rubber and teak too. At one time it was called 'The Rice Bowl of Southeast Asia'. This formerly wealthy country was now reduced to a level of poverty that almost equalled Cambodia. I observed the title of a book for sale near the jewels. It was called *Burma's Struggle against British Imperialism*.

'Good morning, madam.' The loud Burmese voice behind me made me jump. I turned round to face a stern looking armed soldier. 'What are you doing?' he asked. 'I'm just looking around before going for a walk through the gardens,' I replied. 'It's very early,' he said. 'And you are not allowed to walk in the gardens without your guide.' 'I'm only going through the gardens and along the lakeside before I have my breakfast,' I told him as I walked through the door into the bright morning sunshine. After a poor night my nerves were rather edgy and I tried to calm myself down by walking along the lake.

It was a beautiful quiet morning with the sunlight shimmering on the water. The only movement was that of a few water birds fishing for their breakfast. Tropical trees bordering the paths were in blossom, and crows cawed lazily in their heights. I came to the swimming pool and noticed that it was green with algae. As I walked I met a workman slowly sweeping the paths. Greeting him in Burmese in a well practised phrase, 'Good day, how are you?' I was surprised and amused when he replied with a long sentence of which I had no understanding of at all. I smiled in reply and sat down on a seat under a tree to relax in the morning sun. On returning to the hotel I passed the armed soldier on the door, then noticed two pretty women at the reception desk. I asked if I could have my door lock attended to and changed some travellers cheques into kyatts.

The breakfast menu had a 'Sunday Special' of glutinous rice and unpronounceable fish. I decided to try it as a change from dry toast and sweet coffee. But, after struggling for a while to get my fork into the hard dark brown fish, and finding the glutinous rice was almost as tough, I settled for the usual toast! As I was leaving the dining room the smartly dressed girl was waiting for me. 'I'm taking you to the Shwe Dagon

Pagoda today,' she said pleasantly.

'Thank you very much but it is Sunday. It's my day of rest and I don't make other people work on that day either, except, of course, to mend the lock on my door,' I replied.

'Your door doesn't work?' she asked.

'No,' I told her, 'and I'm not prepared to sleep another night with a door that doesn't lock because I have some expensive camera equipment with me. Please would you ensure that this gets done today.'

She talked to the receptionist and they both promised that it would be attended to straight-away. Then she asked, 'Where are you going today?'

'To church,' I replied. 'This government you were telling me about yesterday, that has done so much for the people, also says there is freedom of worship. Is that correct?'

She agreed. I thanked her for her help and she arranged to come back to collect me for the return flight on the next day.

Ronnie arrived punctually and greeted me warmly before driving to church. I relaxed happily and I sat down in the large crowded hall, feeling a great sense of safety and oneness with these lovely Burmese Christians. A gentle breeze blew through the open windows as we sang the first hymn in Burmese:

Jesus keep me near the Cross:
There a precious fountain,
Free to all, a healing stream
Flows from Calvary's mountain.

In the Cross, In the Cross
Be my glory ever;
'til my raptured soul shall find
Rest beyond the river.

(Fanny Crosby)

A German doctor who was sitting next to me offered to translate the service into English. Afterwards he told me he had spent many years living in Burma and he spoke the language fluently. I watched Ronnie speaking to several sick and disabled people as they boarded a mini bus, then he came back to ask me to his home for lunch. I had a most enjoyable afternoon with this remarkable man and his delightful wife, enjoyable even though they told me something of the dangers and difficulties that they face each day. 'We do all we can to obey the authorities,' Ronnie said, 'but with the oppression the people face now, we never know what will happen to us next. There are more and more poor and destitute people as food prices have escalated. We care for them as best we can and God is faithful, supplying all our needs.' It was a privilege to share in the meeting of needs and to learn how much practical help and prayer was appreciated.

At dinner in the hotel that evening a number of Japanese businessmen sat at one table and a small group of American tourists at another. I was reading the menu when an English man touched my shoulder. 'Excuse me, but are you dining alone?' he asked politely. 'Yes, I am,' I replied. 'Do join me if you like.' He sat down and introduced himself, passing me his business card which showed him to be high in the banking world. As we ate, he told me he had been to the northern part of Burma on business.

'Aren't you scared of being here alone?' my companion asked.

'Yes, to a certain extent I am,' I replied.

'I've been here several times,' he said, 'but this visit has made me feel very frightened. Have you seen all the tanks in Rangoon and the armed soldiers on every street?'

'Yes, I have,' I told him. 'And when I returned to my room today I was sure that it had been searched. My belongings had been moved,' I went on.

'What are you doing here?' he enquired. I told him what had first brought me to Burma and how I now had many good friends in the Christian community. 'We have a Chinese girl who is part of our family at home,' he said. 'Our lives have been greatly enriched through her and she has made remarkable progress in her studies.' After a pause he continued, 'I'm making plans to move out of here tomorrow. I'll feel safer at the Strand Hotel as it's nearer the British Embassy.'

I laughed and said, 'Haven't you heard that it is infested with rats? This place only has giant cockroaches!'

We had a pleasant evening together. I was glad to be in the company of someone who shared my compassion for the Burmese people. Since that time both the Strand and the Inya Lake hotels have been renovated. They are now luxury hotels.

As my flight to Bangkok did not leave until Monday afternoon, I took a taxi to visit Stephen and Christopher's uncle, hoping to deliver some gifts Christopher sent for him. Having expected a rather cold reception after their hostility to me on my previous visit, I was pleasantly surprised when they seemed glad to see me. I brought them up to date with the boys' news and asked how they were keeping. They told me that while they had great hopes for their country's future when the League for Democracy won the general election, their hopes had been dashed when the leader, Aung San Suu Kyi, was put under house arrest and the other leaders imprisoned. Things were getting difficult, they explained. New rules made house owners responsible for the upkeep of their roads and the cleanliness of the drains.

Government officers checked the roads and, if they thought they were unsatisfactory, the residents were fined. The uncle had recently undergone major surgery. Following the operation his wife had brought him home to be nursed as conditions at the hospital were unhygienic.

I returned to the hotel feeling sad that the delightful people in this beautiful country were held captive by a regime that appears to bring only poverty and fear. The church, however, was growing under persecution and the services I attended had a beauty and quality I have never experienced in England. While we in Britain have freedom, democracy and a good standard of living for the average person, with these privileges has come godlessness, materialism and a decline in moral standards. Even in the church few care about the needs of their brethren in these difficult lands. While we debate and argue over issues that have clear guidelines in the Bible, we forget our brothers and sisters who are still suffering under dictatorship and communism.

It was a great privilege to move to Sisaket in Thailand, and spend a little time with SAO missionaries Mark and Angela Timmins. These servants of the Lord have seen the fruits of their labours in a thriving church with a Thai pastor. They began their missionary work in the

Cambodian refugee camps about the time we first became involved with our refugees in England. 'Jesus said to his disciples, "The harvest is plentiful but the workers are few"' (Matthew 9:37). We are not all called to work on the overseas mission field, but the Great Commission applies to us all, wherever we serve. Jesus said, 'All authority in heaven and on earth has been given to me. Therefore go and make disciples of all nations, baptising them in the name of the Father and of the Son and of the Holy Spirit and teaching them to obey everything I have commanded you. And surely I will be with you always, to the very end of the age' (Matthew 28:18-20).

CHAPTER FOURTEEN

DEFEAT AND RE-DEDICATION

It was good to be back in England despite the grey skies and pouring rain that greeted me at Heathrow. Lionel met me off the plane and we drove through the wooded lanes to our home. I was amazed at the number of fallen trees that lay along the road sides, the result of a gale that had hit the area in my absence.

That evening I telephoned Christopher to give him news of Burma. He sounded down and depressed. I asked him what was wrong. 'Mum,' he told me sadly, 'my wife got her British passport and yesterday she left me. I just can't believe she could do this to me.'

'Chris, I am really very sorry,' I said. 'What can we do to help? Can you come for the weekend, then we can talk this over?'

He thought for a moment. 'I'd like to come and see you and Dad,' he admitted. 'There is so much to talk about. I'd rather sit down with you than go into details over the phone.' We arranged to have the weekend together.

I thought back over the tragedies that had come into Christopher's life and felt there must be a reason for them all. Perhaps, I concluded, God was training him in the school of hard discipline so that he could help others in the future.

When Chris arrived he looked pale and thin. As we sat together in the study he told us all that had happened. The details are best untold, suffice it to say that he was put upon in the most appalling way. When we heard what Chris had endured, and saw his distress, we felt extremely angry and decided to report the circumstances to the authorities.

'I'm a Christian,' Chris said, through his tears. 'When I gave my testimony at language school I felt so close to God and my life was happy. But I was so upset when I couldn't go on seeing the girl I loved, that's why I became involved with my wife. I keep remembering I'm a Christian and that I've married a Buddhist. The Bible tells us not to marry unbelievers. I've disobeyed God,' he concluded with deep regret. I remembered my missionary friends telling me that Buddhism is a stronghold of Satan and those who are converted from that religion are often targeted by the enemy who seeks to destroy the children of God.

Chris came with us to London that Sunday evening and we all listened to a heart-searching sermon on Christ's second coming. The world is full of wars, rumours of wars, hatred, famine and earthquakes, all predicted in the Bible as signs of the end times. When he comes, what will he find us doing – living carelessly as those who have forgotten him or working in his service and waiting eagerly for his return? The message challenged me afresh. As we drove home Chris said quietly, 'I've a lot to sort out, Mum and Dad. Thanks for standing by me.' We said goodbye with heavy hearts, knowing how badly hurt he was by the break-up of his marriage.

I had gone to sleep when the telephone rang just before midnight. It was Chris. Again the details cannot be shared, but what he found on his return home broke his heart still further. I wondered what more the devil could do in his effort to destroy this orphan. 'Have you any friends nearby?' I asked, feeling so helpless. 'Yes, there's a nice family I know from work,' he said. 'Well, telephone them and ask if you can go there just for a few days until we get something sorted out,' I suggested. 'If they can't have you, ring me back.' I heard nothing more. Lionel and I prayed that God would take care of Chris in a special way as he faced such difficult circumstances. The greatest weapon we have against the devil is prayer; a reality we have proved so many times in our care for these orphans.

1990 passed quickly, as my time was well occupied with meetings at which I showed the audiovisual films on World Vision's work. Business problems loomed large, making me think that I would probably never again visit my dear friends in the Far East. Then one day a letter arrived from Vietnam, from the pastor at Hai's church, telling of outreach work on the Cambodian borders. Because there were so many converts, they had opened two more churches in that area. He was very encouraged by the steady interest in the faith within his own congregation, and forty new members had been added. But they had a problem, a serious shortage of Bibles. He concluded by asking us to pray about this need and also for their safety. Because of the increase in numbers attending church they were experiencing some harassment from government officers. The letter arrived when I was busy helping my husband with some complex business problems. I put it in a drawer intending to read it again later.

In the spring of 1991 we went to the Highlands of Scotland for a holiday. We had never been to that part of Scotland before. We were pleased to find that the cottage was situated in a quiet valley with a fast flowing trout stream running through the garden. Daffodils lined the banks of the stream and, in the adjoining meadows, lambs skipped in the spring sunshine. There were dark green forests where deer roamed and, in the distance, snowcapped mountains soared into the blue skies. It was a perfect location. We enjoyed long walks during the days, and in the evenings we sat in front of a blazing log fire. I had brought some unanswered letters to deal with, including the one from the pastor. 'What have you done about this?' Lionel asked, when he had read it. 'Nothing,' I replied. 'I don't think we're in a position to help just now. Do you?' Lionel thought about it. 'We can't ignore a plea from fellow Christians who need Bibles. Let's contact some Christian organisations when we get back home and see if they know of anyone who's going to Vietnam in the near future.' As we had received no letter from Hai, when I replied to the pastor's letter I asked him to let me know if my friend had gone to America.

Among the unanswered letters there was one that puzzled me. It was from the Director of World Concern in Malaysia. He said they were working in the Sungei Besi Refugee Camp in Kuala Lumpur and that there were some refugees in the camp who had recently fled persecution in Vietnam. One of these refugees had given him my address. The writer, who had heard of my work, asked if I was considering going to Malaysia. I wrote saying I was not considering going to the Far East but, if I could use my experience with the British Refugee Council to help in any way, I would be only too pleased to do so.

Not long after we returned home from holiday, Christopher phoned us with bad news.

His business had run into serious difficulty and he had had to wind it up. He told us that he had left God out of his life again, and that he now wished to rededicate his life as a Christian. We promised to pray that he would not only get employment but also find a suitable place to worship. God heard and answered our prayers. Christopher was successful in getting another job, and on his first day at work, his supervisor told him he was a Christian and invited him to go to his church. A month later Chris phoned and told me he had rededicated his life to the Lord and was proving God's care in so many practical ways. The basic necessities in his home were provided by the Christians he met at church. A Christian financial advisor and a solicitor who were also in the fellowship were prepared to help him sort things out. His faith was being built up by pursuing a Bible study course in his spare time. He also attended a prayer meeting regularly.

The devil had taken him into the pit of despair by whispering that it didn't matter about obeying Bible teaching, undermining him with such thoughts as: you don't need to keep the Sabbath and worship God, you can go into partnership with unbelievers and your business will thrive, it's all right for Christians to marry unbelievers, and if you leave God out of your life you can do just what you want.

When I look back at the time when Christopher's hopes of a Christian marriage were crushed by cruel prejudice, I realise that I was the absent Samaritan in his life, too busy to give him the support he needed. In the parable of the man who fell into the hands of robbers who stripped him, beat him and left him half dead, the first person to see this man in all his need was a priest and he just walked past. Perhaps he was too busy. The second was a Levite; someone who was supposed to serve God. Yet he too ignored the injured man. A Samaritan in those days was someone whom Jews regarded as a second class citizen and not to be associated with. Yet, when a Samaritan came upon the wounded man, he bandaged up his wounds, pouring in oil and wine to disinfect and soothe them. What a description of the depths of human concern, but how much deeper is God's love and compassion that heals the wounds of the sin-sick soul.

If anyone reading this book has experienced some deep hurt: an untimely death, a distressing divorce or the humiliation of a sudden redundancy at work, Christ can come into all these situations with healing and hope for a new beginning. Through him believers are given strength to face difficulties, his hand to hold in the dark, and the promise that he never fails to keep. 'Never will I leave you; never will I forsake you' (Hebrews 13:5). We can use the experience of going through dark valleys hand in hand with the Lord to help others, allowing us to be good Samaritans to them. There is no greater life than to be in the Master's service, bringing his love and care to those in need.

But back to the letter about Bibles. I contacted a number of Christian organisations to see if any of their representatives were going to Vietnam. One replied promptly, asking me to go and see them. I did. But when I showed them the letter from Vietnam they said as it was only one pastor writing, and as he was not on their list, they were not interested. Early July brought another plea from Vietnam. In the same post was a letter from World Concern in Malaysia offering to put a furnished flat at my disposal should I decide to visit the refugee camp. That same week Scripture Gift Mission phoned to ask if I was considering going to Burma in the near future. They had the film ready for printing Bible portions for the Lisu tribe and had obtained permission to print it in Rangoon. Because parcels into Burma often go astray, the safe arrival of important items is only guaranteed if they are taken personally.

Lionel and I discussed the possibility of another Far East visit, but finance was an obstacle. Then he reminded me that over the years I had saved money for a rainy day, never withdrawing anything out of the account. Could that be used? I telephoned an agent for an estimate of the cheapest flights to Thailand, Burma, Vietnam and Malaysia. Meanwhile I phoned the building society to find out how much I could withdraw without jeopardising the long-term interest account. The sum available exactly matched the cost of the air fares.

I prayed and read God's Word for direction, feeling increasingly that God was asking me to return. Taking this as his will, I applied for visas and wrote to the pastor in Vietnam with a provisional date on which I hoped to arrive with Bibles. But how could I help in the situation in Malaysia, especially as I felt reluctant to add additional costs to the trip unless it could be justified? At the end of the same week we went to All Souls Church, Langham Place in London, to hear the first of a special series of sermons. It was a hot summer evening and the heavy traffic caused us to be a little late for the service. The church was packed and we could not find a spare seat. A steward found a seat for me in one part of the building, while Lionel was shown to another. I sat down.

'Hello,' said the man next to me. 'I'm George. I don't think I've seen you here before. Where do you come from?'

I told him we usually came to this special series of meetings each year and that we lived in Burnham. He was not English and I couldn't guess his nationality. 'Do you mind me asking you which country you come from?' I asked.

'Not at all,' he replied happily. 'I'm Malaysian. I come from Kuala Lumpur. This is my wife,' he said, introducing the lady next to him. 'She works for the Chief Administrator of the United Nations High Commission for Refugees in Kuala Lumpur.'

I greeted her and said, 'How very interesting. I'm currently planning a visit to Kuala Lumpur. I've been asked to visit the Sungei Besi Refugee Camp.'

'That's a remarkable coincidence,' the woman replied. 'The Chief Administrator is in London for a few days this week. I'll introduce you to her and you can have a chat.'

It was a challenging sermon on the urgency of the times we live in and the need to spread the Christian gospel to every corner of the world. The following week I ordered twenty Vietnamese Bibles from the Bible Society, asking for a letter of authorisation in case of problems at customs. Scripture Gift Mission sent me three hundred Bible portions in Vietnamese. Having been given these encouragements, I sent a circular letter to the churches in my area inviting them to help with the needs in Vietnam. By a week before my flight to Bangkok I had nearly £700 to take to the church there.

After packing my suitcase I weighed it. Even with the very minimum of personal belongings it was obviously overweight. A quick call to the airline confirmed that I would have to pay an excess baggage charge of £240. As I was on a tight budget for this trip I prayed that this charge would be waived at both Heathrow and Bangkok. And I had another matter for prayer. There was a problem regarding my Burmese visa. But I felt so clearly that the hand of God was over this trip that I was not unduly worried when I flew out of Heathrow without it.

CHAPTER FIFTEEN

THE WAY OF THE CROSS IN VIETNAM

The excess baggage charge was waived at Heathrow when I explained why my luggage was so heavy. After a long tedious flight I checked into my hotel room in Bangkok, exhausted. Immediately the telephone rang. It was the Burmese office of my travel agency, asking me to go there at once as there was a problem with my visa. Wearily I got into a taxi and went to the office. Although I showed the travel clerk the visa approval that had gone to the Embassy in London, he insisted that I had to start the application again, explaining that many visa applications were being refused. When I asked what the chances were of my application being successful, he said they were fifty fifty. As I was flying to Vietnam first, he agreed to photocopy my passport and put the application into the Embassy in Bangkok while I was in Vietnam.

I returned to the hotel only to hear the telephone ringing in my room yet again. This time it was the Vietnamese agent, who informed me that my flights to and from Vietnam were on stand-by only and could not be guaranteed. I phoned very good friends in Bangkok who were involved in mission work there. Paul and Lois

Jenks had been missionaries in Thailand for many years. Paul introduced himself to me on my first visit to the Bangkok Evangelical Church. He was an elder there. The Jenks lead their mission, Advancing the Ministries of the Gospel. They work primarily in child care and have orphanages, child care centres and feeding centres. Most importantly they show the love of Jesus Christ to needy people throughout Thailand, Albania, Greece, Russia and many Asian countries. Like me they had a great interest in Burma. They agreed to join me for dinner the next evening. I unpacked and went straight to bed, tired out but confident that God would see me through these difficulties. And that is what he did. My flights to Vietnam were confirmed the next day and I enjoyed the evening with Paul and Lois. When I told them about the problem with the Burmese visa, and that if it was not granted all my flights would have to be rescheduled, they kindly offered me a room in their home if that should happen. Their promise to pray, both for my visit to Vietnam and over my Burmese visa, greatly cheered me. We arranged to meet again on my return from Vietnam.

When I checked in for the Vietnam flight, it was with a heavy case and laden overnight bag. This was no wonder, as I was carrying a set of communion cups and some basic medical supplies which were very expensive in Vietnam. When the airport staff raised their eyebrows and told me I had about three hundred dollars to pay, I explained that I was visiting Christians in Vietnam and taking them Bibles and medical supplies. 'You're a kind lady!' the officer said, waving me through to the departure lounge.

On completing the custom forms at Ho Chi Minh City Airport, a customs officer called me into his office. He told me to show him the Bibles I had declared. I did so, also producing the letter of authorisation from the Hong Kong Bible Society. Two other customs officers came into the room and searched all my bags. 'You are not allowed to bring in Bibles,' I was informed. I asked why they had made such a rule when the Bible taught people to obey the government. I showed them Romans Chapter 13 and asked them to read it. When they had read the chapter, they asked about the scripture portions in my luggage. I explained that these were portions of the Bible, not any kind of political propaganda. After a lengthy discussion, they kept eighteen of the twenty Bibles and one hundred scripture portions. One of them issued me with a receipt, saying I could collect all the remaining literature at a customs office in Saigon on the Monday providing I took one of my friends with me.

I was disappointed at this turn of events, as I had felt sure these Bibles would be safe. When I got to the hotel it was small, comfortable and the staff were very friendly. I asked the receptionist if she would arrange a taxi to take me to Hai's address, having heard that he was still in Saigon. The driver had difficulty in finding the house, but we finally got there after travelling for two hours in the dark. There is very little street lighting outside the city and finding places presents a problem. Hai greeted me happily, but said quietly that he did not think it was wise to say too much when the taxi driver was listening. He promised to take a message to the church leaders, telling them where I was staying in order that they could meet me in the morning. As it was late we arranged to speak again in the church. After our brief conversation I left Hai and returned to the taxi.

It was the monsoon season and the journey was made more difficult because the pot-holed roads were now full of water. The night was dark and the rain lashed down in torrents. As I looked out of the car window searching for buildings I recognised from previous visits, I suddenly saw a large cross in the black sky. It appeared to be illuminated in dark red. Straining to see where it was, I supposed it to be on the roof of a church. I watched this cross for some while as we travelled along the flooded roads. And words of Jesus came into my mind. 'If anyone would come after me, he must deny himself and take up his cross and follow me. For whoever wants to save his life will lose it, but whoever loses his life for me will find it' (Matthew 16:24-25). The dark red cross suddenly disappeared. I thought of my first visit to the church in Saigon, remembering the beauty of the service and the obvious dedication of the people. 'Take up your cross,' Jesus tells us, and we must do this if we really want to follow him. It is so easy to be a follower of Christ in Britain, but what do we really know about denying ourselves or suffering because we have chosen to follow the way of the cross?

It was nearly midnight when I finally reached the hotel. Having unpacked, I read that challenging Bible passage and prayed. I asked God to guide me to church in the morning. Packing the remaining Bibles, scripture portions and other gifts into my overnight bag to take with me to the church in the morning, I called it a day and went to bed.

Waking very early the following morning, I read for a while then decided to have an early breakfast. The dining room was on the top floor of the hotel and had a small balcony on which guests could sit in the sun. The breakfast buffet was beautifully presented and the food interesting. I had a glass of coconut milk, fresh pineapple and mango, then some crisp French bread with coffee. As I did not know what arrangements had been made regarding going to church, I wandered down to the reception at 7.15am. There was no one at the desk.

'Mrs. Brenda,' a voice said quietly. I looked round and there, by the entrance, were two men from the church. How glad I was to see them. When we went outside one of them said, 'We are so pleased to see you. God has sent you to us at this time. Please may we ask you not to take a taxi? We have borrowed motor bikes to come here. Our lives are very difficult and we are being watched so please would you mind coming with me on the motor bike?' Having collected my heavily laden bag, and feeling rather nervous, I got on the back of one of the small motor bikes while the other rider strapped my bag on to the back of his.

The skies were blue and it was a hot day after the storm and the rain of the previous evening, but the roads were still very flooded. We wound our way around the pot-holes and I hung on to the rider as the motor bike swerved and skidded in the mud. For the very first time I wished I had worn trousers to church! It took quite a lot of concentration to keep a grip on the foot rests with high heeled shoes! Eventually, as we approached an area that looked just a sea of mud, I closed my eyes and prayed that we would reach the church safely. The nine miles to the Hoc Mon district seemed a very long journey. But we arrived safely, and I was more than a little surprised to find no mud on either my shoes or dress!

Hai, who was waiting to greet me, introduced me to Nga, a Christian lady. We went into the church and sat down to chat before the service. He told me there was a delay over him leaving Vietnam because his mother had been very ill. She had died a month before. Hai had remained to be with her and attend her funeral. Much had happened to him since we had last met. He had grown in the faith, being well taught at the church. In God's goodness he had met Nga, and they were to be married the following month.

The church filled up and the service began with a really joyful rendering of the lovely hymn of faith:

I know not why God's wondrous grace
To me He hath made known
Nor why unworthy, Christ in love
Redeemed me for His own
But I know whom I have believed
And am persuaded that He is able
To keep that which I've committed
Unto Him against that day.

I know not when my Lord may come
At night or noon day fair
Nor if I'll walk the vale with Him
Or 'meet Him in the air."
But I know whom I have believed...

(El Nathan)

There was no organ or piano accompanying the singing, the people are far too poor to think of buying such luxuries. The pastor who had led the worship on my previous visit was not there. A younger man preached, giving a very serious word on the pathway of the Christian being the way of the cross and the need for everyone to understand that our redemption has been bought with a price, the blood of Jesus. The cross stands at the crossroads of every life, we were reminded, and we have to walk the narrow way of obedience and service to him if we would experience the joy and happiness of a life of victory.

Later in the service, a young man walked on to the platform and the older men stood round him with their hands on his shoulders. I asked Hai what this was all about. 'He's our new deputy pastor,' he whispered. 'They're committing him to God and he's promising to serve God throughout his life in easy ways, hard ways, suffering, prison and perhaps a martyr's death.'

'A deputy pastor, Hai, why do you need a deputy pastor?' I enquired.

'Mrs. Brenda, don't you know?' Hai said with deep emotion. 'The pastor who led me to Christ was arrested a month ago and he's in prison. I don't know if I'll see him again.' Tears rolled down his cheeks as he told me this news. I had not heard, probably because not all letters get past the censor.

As the service was coming to an end, a lady went to the microphone and spoke earnestly to the congregation. 'That's our pastor's wife,' Hai explained. 'She's asking everyone to pray for the release of her husband and she's reminding us that we must all continue in the faith and follow Christ.' I watched this woman of faith as she opened her hymn book and began to sing a beautiful song of praise. At first her voice shook with emotion, but before she finished, her praise echoed throughout the church building, leaving an impression on me that I shall never forget.

After the service the retired pastor came over to greet me. 'I'm very sorry we cannot ask you to bring us a greeting as we did last year,' he said. 'Now we are not allowed to have visitors on the platform. There are government officers who watch us. Please pray for our safety.' The imprisoned pastor's wife gave me a warm welcome too. 'Please can you help?' she asked. 'Will you tell your church members in England we need their prayers? Do they know what life is like for us in this Communist country? Every day we walk in fear, not knowing what will happen to us. But we do know our God can save us.'

I asked if there was any chance of getting permission to visit her husband, but she explained that only she had permission to visit him once a month and that the prison was sixty miles away. Because the expense of getting there was high, the church members were helping her. I promised her I would do all I could to help.

The old pastor asked if I would like to go back to his house with other church leaders. Would Hai come too? No, he dared not. It might prejudice his chance of freedom. Before leaving the church Hai told me he now had a date to go to America, and that Nga would accompany him as his wife. I said goodbye to Hai and Nga, promising to contact him when they had moved to America. 'It will be a very big change for me,' he said as we parted. 'My children won't know me. I've very few possessions to take in my suitcase. But my most valuable possession doesn't need packing. It's my faith in God.'

It was only a short distance from the church to the house and I travelled again on the back of the bike. Most of the roads in the area were thick with mud and the homes extremely poor. Courtyards surrounding the homes housed large earthenware water pots as there was no water on tap. The pastor had a very primitive supply of electricity for lighting and operating the fan in the living room. He and his wife very warmly welcomed me into their home and I was glad to sit with them and hear all that had happened. They told me that there had been eighty-six new converts since my last visit and that government officers had come to some of the services.

Although he never spoke against the government, the old man's licence to preach had been taken away.

One month before my visit their house was surrounded by armed police late at night. They forced open the door and ordered everyone out on to the road. One of them shouted, 'Which is Pastor Q?' On identifying himself, the old man was forced into a waiting car and taken to prison without charge or trial. When his wife visited him she found the prison conditions very bad, but was heartened to discover that her husband was witnessing to the other prisoners. The house in which I was a guest was very overcrowded. It was little wonder. Because some preachers' homes had been confiscated, they all lived together with the old pastor and his wife.

I opened my bag and took out two Bibles, explaining that I had brought twenty altogether and that a church member had to accompany me to the custom's office the next day if we were to retrieve them. Worried about their safety, I asked them if there would be repercussions. So delighted were they with the two Bibles that I could not get them to answer my question at first! When I showed them the rest of the contents of my bag, and gave them the gifts from the churches, the people were quite overwhelmed. Their joy made the whole trip worthwhile.

The pastor's son volunteered to accompany

me to customs. I showed them the receipt and the address and asked if it would make any trouble for them. 'Did you declare the Bibles?' the pastor asked. 'Yes,' I replied, 'they were all on my customs form.' 'That's good,' he said. 'If you had smuggled them we'd be in trouble.' 'Are you likely to have problems after my visit?' I enquired. The pastor's son translated for his father. 'Mrs. Brenda, as Christians we walk the way of the cross. Our future path we do not know, but God is with us. He will keep us.' Having arranged to meet me the next day, the young man took me back to the hotel on his motor bike. I looked carefully to see if there were any church buildings along the route but there were none to be seen. The area was flat, poverty stricken, and with only a few shops among the dilapidated houses. As I ate my dinner that night I thought of all the churches in Britain where we can meet together without fear, yet our faith is so weak and many of our churches are half empty.

The pastor's son met me at the customs office in the morning. There was a lot of people queuing to collect videos, cigarettes and alcohol. When our turn came the officer looked at us both, then asked me for my passport and visa. 'How did you meet this man?' he demanded harshly. 'He's a Christian as I am,' I replied quietly. 'What's your name and address?' he asked the pastor's son, writing down the details. 'Come back next week with your passport and visa and you can have all the items on the receipt,' we were told. I explained that I would be in Burma by then.

'Why is it,' I asked, 'that while we have waited in the queue people have taken away videos, cigarettes and alcohol? The items I am asking to be released are good books that show people how to lead good honest lives.' The man grew quite angry and told us to leave. I asked my companion to come back to the hotel for a snack.

'I'm very disappointed about the Bibles,' I said as we ate. 'Will you be safe to go back next week?'

'I will definitely go back,' he assured me. 'But what will I do without your passport?'

'That's a problem,' I agreed. 'But I have an idea. I've a very nice guide this time. If I explain the situation to him and ask him to accompany you, would that be acceptable?'

'That's a good idea,' the man said eagerly. 'Tell him what's happened.'

My guide arrived very promptly and I explained the situation to him. He took my passport and visa, photographed and returned them, then promised to accompany the pastor's son the following week. I thanked him very much for taking so much care. When I said goodbye to the pastor's son I asked him to write to me and let me know what happened. Packing my few belongings in my half empty case, I readied myself for the flight back to Bangkok. As I boarded the small aircraft I thought of the lives of the Christians I was leaving behind. They were so poor in the world's terms yet rich in faith. Their commitment to Christ could take them to prison or death or leave them living in uncertainty about what the future would bring. Yet their faith was firmly grounded in the God of the Bible, the God who would never leave them nor forsake them. Caring for my two Vietnamese refugees had put me in touch with these heroic twentieth century saints, saints unknown to most of the world yet well known in heaven.

CHAPTER SIXTEEN

A CALL FROM KUALA LUMPUR

I flew back to Bangkok the next day and found a message for me at the hotel instructing me to go to the Burmese travel agent. 'We have your visa approval and will take your passport to the Embassy today to be stamped,' the clerk said, when I arrived in the office. 'As this is just a short visit, there are certain regulations you must keep. My agent will meet you at Rangoon airport and you're not allowed to travel anywhere without permission. You're very lucky to get a visa,' he went on. 'We've arranged tours for several groups this year and the authorities in Rangoon have cancelled their applications at the last minute for no reason. We'll bring your passport to the hotel this evening.'

I went back to my hotel to ring Paul and Lois who were to join me for dinner that evening. As they employed Ronnie's son in their office, they were kept up to date on what was happening in Burma. When they arrived I told them the good news about my visa. 'We've be praying that you would get it, because we've a job for you. While you were in Vietnam there have been huge storms and floods in the southern delta of Burma. Whole villages were washed away and there are thousands of homeless, sick people needing urgent help. We faxed our head office and were pleased to be granted $5000 worth of basic medicines and food packs. We want you to go in and get Ronnie to organise the relief programme.' I said that I'd be delighted to do that. The rest of the evening was spent talking about Vietnam. My friends told me that they would ensure that news of the hardships and persecution there was circulated to all their contacts to encourage them to pray, both for the day to day problems and for the pastor's release from prison.

It was a pleasant surprise to pass through customs in Rangoon without any interrogation. The travel guide knew I visited Burma regularly and had several friends in Rangoon. I told her that over the years I had grown very attached to the Burmese people. Ronnie and his wife joined me for dinner. We enjoyed each other's company and were able to discuss the flood relief programme. Because the authorities refused to admit there was a disaster, very few people outside the country knew about it. General Ne Win, the country's backstage ruler, is a very superstitious man. Any natural disasters are regarded as the spirits being angry with him. He therefore ignores them.

Ronnie had arranged to collect me for church, and I sat in the hotel reception waiting for him.

As I waited, I read an outstanding book on the life of Adoniram Judson, the first missionary to take the gospel to Burma. His life was one of intense suffering, but the Lord blessed his work in a remarkable way. When Ronnie walked through the entrance with his usual beaming smile, he observed the book. Picking it up, he asked, 'Have you read the account of the first convert to Christianity?' 'Yes, I have,' I replied. 'Show me the page where it records that first convert,' Ronnie said. I found it quickly. 'You see his name, Brenda. That man was my great grandfather. Every male down the line has been a Christian and church leader. Burma owes so much to Judson's pioneer work.'

While we travelled, I asked Ronnie how his congregation was progressing. He told me that they had new converts every month and that the total number of members was now one thousand one hundred and twenty-one. When we arrived at the church I saw outside it a large red cross on a white board. My friend explained that this symbol was being used throughout the country wherever Christians were praying for the flood victims. It also marked the church building as a reception centre at which people could give money, clothing and food for the relief programme.

The church was crowded and about fifty people stood outside listening to the service through the open windows. Ronnie was preaching that morning and I watched his face light up with joy as he brought the gospel message to the people. His enthusiasm and zeal for the Lord was infectious and, when he finished, his compassionate heart was evident as he spoke firstly to the poor, the sick and disabled and then to everyone else.

Just caring for two Anglo-Burmese orphans had brought me into contact with this exemplary man whose life radiated with the reflection of Christ. When Stephen and Christopher first arrived in our home it never crossed my mind that through them I would make such valuable contacts in Burma.

On leaving Rangoon the aeroplane took a route over the flooded delta area. I thought of the people there who had lost their homes, praying that they would now be reached with the gospel and cared for practically. God's heart of love must be demonstrated through his people in situations such as that. And when we do that I believe it makes him glad. The plane landed at Singapore, but as there was insufficient time to transfer my luggage to the on-going flight to Kuala Lumpur, I had to wait for the next flight. Although it was after midnight when I arrived, the Director of World Concern met me at the airport and took me to the flat that they had provided.

Sungei Besi Camp was about ten miles outside the city and it held twelve thousand Vietnamese refugees. I toured it with one of the aid workers. We visited the small, clean and well equipped hospital. The doctor there told me some of the refugees arriving in the camp had a very virulent form of tuberculosis that was becoming increasingly difficult to treat. A young man of twenty-four had died of the disease that week. Most of the buildings housing the refugees were wooden structures. I was particularly impressed by the crafts that were being made in the workshop. One aid worker who taught the refugees English, supervised the workroom. My escort told me the work in the camp was difficult and at times very frustrating as a large majority of the refugees were economic migrants and the stories they told to get refugee status were lies.

The Camp Commandant asked me to go to his office for a talk. 'What is your interest in the Vietnamese refugee problem?' he asked. I told him that I had worked on a voluntary basis for British Refugee Council, helping on the resettlement programme when Britain first took in Vietnamese refugees after the Vietnam war. 'I'm impressed with your level of care. Have you been to Vietnam?' he asked. I told him that I had visited Vietnam on three occasions and shared with him a little of my experiences with the church there. 'I'm a Muslim,' the Camp

Commandant said, 'but these experiences are very important to us at this time. We have some refugees applying for asylum on the grounds of persecution of their faith. I would like you to meet them and I'll arrange an interpreter. One particular refugee is currently on an island camp. She's coming here on Friday and I want you to meet her.'

Our conversation continued. 'May I ask you to type a report on your visits to Vietnam, especially the details of what you found on this recent visit?' the Commandant said. 'It's very relevant to our screening procedure. When you have completed it I want you to take it to the Chief Administrator of United Nations High Commission to Refugees in Kuala Lumpur.'

'That's interesting,' I replied, 'because I had a long conversation with her while she was in London just before I came out here.' The Commandant asked how I had been put in touch with her. I told him the details. 'I'm a Muslim,' he concluded, 'but I admit that's a remarkable coincidence!'

Having written the report, I took a taxi to the United Nations High Commission for Refugees and was shown into the Chief Administrator's office. She was a very pleasant woman and seemed genuinely pleased to see me again. We talked for a long time and she read the report. 'I'm a Muslim but these circumstances are quite extraordinary,' she admitted. As I prepared to leave she accompanied me to the entrance door. 'Thank you so much for coming,' the lady said. 'Please come back before you leave and we will have another talk.'

On my next visit to the camp I was introduced to the refugee from Bidong Pulau. As her English was good we needed no interpreter. 'Don't you remember me?' she asked excitedly. 'I translated your message of greeting when you came to our church two years ago.' Only when I looked at the girl again did I recognise her as one of those who had sat on the front row of the Hoc Mon District Church and translated my message. 'Yes, I do!' I told her. 'How did you come to be here?' She told me she had been the Sunday school teacher at the church, and had also given English lessons. Very early one Sunday morning, while she was holding a class, the police arrived. They told her they would arrest her and any others who taught the Christian faith. The police said they would return the following morning. Late that same night she joined a group of Christians and fled in a small boat on the Mekong River. They were taken out to sea and transferred to a larger boat packed with refugees fleeing the country. The boat, which was in a bad state of repair, limped into harbour on the Malaysian coast and all aboard were taken to the Bidong camp.

She asked if I would support her application

for refugee status on the basis of the persecution for her faith, explaining that she was asking for asylum in Canada. I spent the rest of the day talking with her and a small group of Christian refugees. Through an interpreter I pointed out to them what might lie ahead. I told them of the difficulties that had to be overcome when adjusting to a totally new lifestyle: bitterly cold winters, racial tensions, the language barrier, and the difficulties in obtaining employment in countries that already had a high number of people unemployed. I made them aware of the lifelessness in many western churches. Maintaining the faith was not easy, I explained, when living in a society whose goals were materialistic gain, and whose moral standards were low. By the end of a day spent in the cramped and overcrowded conditions of the refugee camp I felt tired and emotionally drained.

I slept badly that night, the thought of these poor refugees wanting a new life in a society like ours preyed on my mind. Was it right to help them start life again in such a different and Christless society? Then I was reminded of my own early years, when I was held in a regime of fear and oppression and had no liberty to live a normal Christian life. Having been freed from that authoritarian rule I was called to care for those seeking freedom.

The following day I went again to the

headquarters of UNHCR in Kuala Lumpur where I completed forms supporting the applications of a very small number of the refugees I had talked with at the camp, including the interpreter from the Hoc Mon District Church in Saigon. When the Chief Administrator took time to speak with me, I told her how torn I felt in the work I did, as the successful resettlement of refugees in a new culture depended on how much support they received from Christians who were called to care.

When I returned to the flat I felt so tired that I prepared a simple meal, then sat on the balcony looking out at the dark skies. The thunder and lightning of a monsoon storm filled the air. Sometimes in the Christian life we feel like a small boat in a storm-tossed sea. The life of faith often hits unseen obstacles and we face the danger of shipwreck. But there is One who walks above the storms of life. He holds out his hands and says, 'It is I, don't be afraid' (John 6:20). I remembered his voice all those years ago, and thought back over the many ways in which I had experienced his guiding hand and loving care.

When, on my return, Lionel met me at Heathrow, I told him that the trip had been the most exhausting one I had done and I needed a few days of rest. But that was not to be. Alison, who was expecting her second baby, was not very well, and before that day was out, she was admitted to hospital. Our little granddaughter, Natalie, who was only two, came to us. At the end of the week Alison was transferred to a London hospital critically ill. Doctors told us that they hoped to save her life but that there was little hope for the baby.

In God's goodness, and in answer to prayer, the baby arrived three and a half months premature, so tiny yet so perfect. Little Tania Rose was in hospital for three months and came home on Christmas Eve. This little child, whom doctors had said would be brain damaged or severely disabled, is the prettiest little girl and today has no health problems at all. What a God we worship and serve!

CHAPTER SEVENTEEN

NEW HOPE FOR CAMBODIA

I joined the Council of Southeast Asian Outreach (SAO) after it had gained entry into Cambodia with aid projects. The first visit I made as a council member was in 1993. SAO had two projects at that time, ophthalmic healthcare and fish farming. Theirs was a holistic ministry, with the gospel message of Christ as the Light of the World and the Bread of Life and practical Christianity going hand in hand. Rev. Jim Verner and his wife, Agnes, WEC missionaries seconded to SAO and with twenty-eight years experience in Thailand, were our Field Directors. Their goal was to see Cambodians won for Christ.

The Headquarters of WEC are near our home and we are privileged to have several WEC workers in our congregation. I was privileged to meet Jim and Agnes in Phnom Penh and felt instantly drawn to them. Jim was born in Castlederg, Co. Tyrone in Northern Ireland. After two years at Bible College he received a clear call from God to work in Cambodia. He was accepted by WEC and commissioned for Cambodia in 1964. The plan was that he would spend five years in Thailand while waiting for

Cambodia to open to missionary work.

While working and studying in Thailand, Jim met Agnes who came from Canada. She had a degree from Bible College and was also a music teacher, language supervisor, youth speaker and leprosy worker. Agnes had even been on radio as violinist with Voice of Peace choir. This remarkably talented couple, who could have commanded high salaries in the secular world, were married with so little money they couldn't afford to buy a wedding ring! Jim and Agnes pioneered an entirely new work in a hitherto unreached area of Sukhothai province in Thailand. Sukhothai had a reputation for bandits, violence and robberies (of which they were victims on several occasions), but God richly blessed the work. Right from the start it was characterised by miracles wrought among spirit worshippers, opium addicts and spirit mediums. Ruthless robbers were wonderfully changed, and the fruit of those first two years of God's direct intervention in the lives of heathen villagers continues growing to this day.

When the Vietnam War and Pol Pot terrors closed the doors of Cambodia to missionaries for many years, Jim and Agnes worked tirelessly in neighbouring Thailand, planting churches and living a basic lifestyle among the people. Jonathan and Sharon were born during the early years of their work and the children's first language was Thai. Jim was also consultant to the Evangelical Fellowship of Thailand for six years and a member of their Administrative Committee for twelve. In 1992, Jim and Agnes studied Khmer in Northeast Thailand with the expectation of a door opening in Cambodia. When the Verners joined SAO their pastoral care was invaluable.

What a memorable day it was for me when I first met them in Phnom Penh, where they accompanied me to an indigenous Cambodian church. Little did I ever think, when I was called to help Cambodian refugees in England, that I would ever have the privilege of worshipping God together with his people in their homeland. The pastor and most of the congregation had endured the terrible hardships of the Khmer Rouge years. It was with deep emotion that I joined with them to sing 'All people that on earth do dwell, sing to the Lord with cheerful voice' (Psalm 100:1, Metrical version).

The singing that day in the Khmer language was beautiful. The thought of their cheerful voices praising God despite the fact that many had lost love ones through torture, starvation, and the terrible war, moved me deeply. What a fine example they are of how the love of Christ triumphs in the face of appalling tragedy. The church had only recently received official recognition, having continued for many years underground. There was a new day dawning for this land that had seen unparalleled suffering in modern times. Churches were opening and precious seeds sown by faithful servants of Christ were now taking root and growing.

I travelled with Nigel and Milet Goddard, both highly qualified aquaculturists, into poor villages to see the work of establishing fish farms. It was fascinating to learn how they had gone about the project. First of all, they surveyed the area to find which waste products were available to feed fish. Then they matched the fish to the waste products. In one very pretty village where there were a few ducks, the fish they introduced into the ponds were chosen because they fed on duck droppings! In another where there were termites, they used fish that fed on termites. This project enabled villagers to supplement their poor diet with nutritious fish at no cost.

The Goddards are both firmly grounded in the faith and, having learned the Khmer language, they are able to share the gospel message as well as give practical help. The Lord has greatly blessed their ministry. Each Saturday at the large Aquaculture Development Centre built by SAO, they, with Jim and Agnes Verner, preach the good news of Jesus to the village people, who listen appreciatively. Nigel and Milet love teaching the children, who are eager and willing to learn. Cambodian children are very attractive. Most of them, having never even seen a toy, play contentedly with stones in the dust, a mangy looking dog and an equally scruffy cat lazing in the sun nearby.

As we chatted in the Land Cruiser on our return to Phnom Penh, I discovered that Nigel had done part of his training at the Veterinary Research Laboratories where I had also been for two years of my medical research training. Both Milet's parents died while she was studying at the Asian Institute of Technology in Bangkok. One of the directors and his wife 'adopted' Milet and helped to nurture her in the faith. She is a beautiful Filipino who has the inner beauty of one who loves the Lord. I asked her about her foster parents and discovered that Milet's foster father was the German doctor who translated for me in the church at Rangoon. Over the years that I have served on SAO's council I learned to love and admire the people God has called to serve him in this land.

Claire Davies, a well-qualified optometrist from Wales, did the foundational optometry work. She pioneered the School of Optometry and trained Khmer staff to continue the facility. Her work widened out to include eye clinics in the rural areas. On my second visit I travelled with Claire to Battambang and watched her helping with an eye clinic run jointly by Help

Age and SAO. So many people at that clinic only required a cataract operation to restore their sight, others merely needed correctly prescribed spectacles.

The people of the province of Battambang had been severely affected by land mines and Claire arranged for me to visit a trauma ward of mine victims. The late Princess Diana rightly drew the land mine problem into world headlines. These terrible weapons of war continue to kill and maim long after wars cease. It is, I believe, imperative that Christians raise their voices when action is needed to protect the poor and vulnerable from much mindless maiming. My tour of the hospital was heartrending. So many children and young people there were permanently disabled and disfigured. In many cases their lives are ruined, as they had no prospect of ever earning a living. The Battambang hospital was well run and relatively clean, but hundreds of land mine victims are taken to rural hospitals where facilities are so poor that they succumb to infection and die. There were two and three-year-old children in the hospital with no legs and missing arms, lying in cots soaked in blood. Their large dark brown eyes looked at me with a helplessness I shall never forget.

There are several provinces in Cambodia that are now quite useless for rice cultivation because of the risk of land mines. This scourge causes food shortages in a country that has difficulty enough feeding its people adequately.

Claire took me to an optometry shop she had established through SAO. The Khmer staff had all been trained in the School of Optometry in Phnom Penh. I noticed a Bible on the table. A Cambodian girl who was skilfully making lenses had an artificial leg. Claire told me she had trained this amputee and told her about the love of Christ. The girl was attending a church in Battambang. While very few amputees have till recently had a chance to earn a living, there are now an increasing number of Aid Agencies helping land mine victims. But at the time of my visit in 1994, an average of one hundred and twenty to one hundred and forty new casualties were brought in each month. The Eye Healthcare Project closed, but the School of Optometry continues to operate under Khmer management.

SAO also teaches handicrafts to returning refugees in order that they can earn a living by their new skills. Marie Cornelius is in charge of this work and I enjoyed a visit to her home. There were looms for weaving silk and I saw a number of refugees busy making silver jewellery, greeting cards and a wide variety of silk products. Marie first worked with YWAM in the refugee camps, where she soon became fluent in Khmer. Her work, which has been remarkably blessed, has resulted in a thriving church in Kirivong.

Agnes Verner established the language school to teach Khmer to missionaries and expatriates. This is now the largest and most successful venture of its kind in Phnom Penh. Jim is building up the national church sound in teaching and doctrine. I have observed this dedicated couple working from early morning until late at night, often seven days a week, yet they retain a great sense of humour whatever pressure they are under.

During my last visit to Cambodia in 1997 I was taken very ill and flown to Thailand, where I was admitted to hospital. In the quietness and solitude of my room I reflected over the years I had been called to care for the people of Southeast Asia. God's loving hand was even over this illness, as the condition brought to light, at a very early stage, pre-cancerous lesions which needed to be removed. My daughter Rosemary, a travel agent, flew out to Thailand and brought me home.

As I unpacked my bags in the comfort of my home I remembered all the Christians I had left behind. Many of them know what it is to live under harsh military dictatorships that rule through fear, or with communist governments which persecute Christians for their faith and bring poverty and destitution in their wake. In Britain we are privileged to have a democratic system that ensures our freedom. But what are we doing with it? The forces of evil are attacking our country: encouraging a decline in discipline, the abolition of censorship, and the forsaking of moral standards. Yet most of us in our freedom watch silently as our society is bound and shackled. By and large the church raises no objection to what is happening, some of its leaders even bend over backwards to accommodate other faiths into their thinking. Yet we have a gospel that saves to the uttermost, cares for the weakest, heals the sin-sick and gives life and purpose for living that can be found in no other way. Why, I wondered, are most of us silent?

Some time later, a letter arrived from Vietnam telling me that the Bibles had been safely collected from customs. Along with their thanks came a plea to me to be a voice in Britain for their suffering church, a voice that would encourage people to intercede for them by reminding my fellow Christians in the western world of Paul's word to the Hebrews, 'Remember those in prison as if you were their fellow prisoners, and those who are ill-treated as if you yourselves were suffering' (Hebrews 13:3).

As I review our extended family I realise how much we have to praise God for, and how many situations need our continued prayers.

Minh, who married a Vietnamese girl he met in America, lives with his wife and little son in Houston. Anh moved to Dallas and, still with that loving heart for her family, she made a return visit to Vietnam to arrange for her elderly mother to move to America to be with her. When she booked her airline tickets, a Vietnamese man working in the travel agency observed her name. He looked at her carefully then said, 'Anh, you and I were at Saigon University together. Do you remember me?' She did. A few months later they decided to marry.

Anh telephoned us in the middle of the night with this exciting news. They had fixed a date for their wedding and wanted Lionel and me to attend. Both our diaries were full, but as we had the weekend free we flew to Dallas for the wedding. It was a beautiful October day and our pretty little Anh made a radiant bride. Perhaps the highlight of the occasion was when Hai and Nga arrived at the wedding reception with Hai's four children.

Anh asked me to give a speech. I was almost speechless with emotion as I told the assembled guests what a wonderful God we serve, and how in his own amazing way he had brought us all together that day. Anh and her husband now have a little son and daughter, but in their busy lives they find no time to attend church. We have loving letters from Anh keeping us informed of family news. We remember them in our prayers. Hai and Nga have settled into a Christian Vietnamese church in Houston and are going on well with the Lord. Anh's mother died just before she was due to leave Vietnam.

Tien, who still lives in London, keeps in touch with us and visits us with his wife and five children. He has returned to Vietnam for several visits but is very happily settled in England and is grateful for the opportunities he has to contribute to our society.

Thida lives with her husband and two children in southeast London. We see them regularly. Thida's husband visited Cambodia in the hope of returning there with his wife and family. Although he was overjoyed to be back in his homeland with all its beauty and tranquillity, he was torn when he saw the violence and poverty. Thida does not wish to return as both children are making excellent progress at school. Thida's husband has been through a long period of despair and depression. He longs to go home but realises that his children would have little hope of a future there as the education system is so poor. His home and family are here but his heart longs to be in Cambodia.

Bopha went to America to visit her grandmother. When she was there she met an American Cambodian whom she later married. Bopha lives in Philadelphia with her husband

and two daughters. She always writes at Christmas.

Christopher's life has taken on a new direction since he returned to the Lord. He has a good job and has married again. His wife, Sandar, who is Burmese and a physics teacher, was a student at Rangoon University with Ponnie. She comes from a Muslim family who live in the London area. Both Christopher and Sandar attend church and Sandar has a real interest in the Christian faith. Lionel and I hope and pray that she will make a firm commitment to Christ.

Stephen and Ponnie, who live very close to us, are both committed Christians. Ponnie has an excellent job in research and is studying for a PhD in her spare time. Stephen enjoys his work in electronics. They both attend church and Ponnie has been a good influence on Stephen. She reminds me of her mother Grace. There are very few Burmese Christians living in England and both Stephen and Christopher are much in need of prayer support, that they will remain true to the Lord.

As both our daughters live within a half hour drive of our home we see them frequently. Russell and Alison are good parents and our granddaughters are a constant source of fun and happiness to us. Little Tania Rose, who had such a grave prognosis at birth, is now a very pretty little girl with no health problems. How we thank

God for hearing and answering our prayers. Natalie is a sweet natured girl who is learning to play the clarinet. I accompany her on the piano and we enjoy our musical evenings together.

Rosemary has her own travel agency in the beautiful old village of Cookham. Although she is a successful businesswoman, she has a heart for those less well off than herself and has been involved with an organisation which provides wells in African villages where no clean water supplies exist.

I am glad that Rosemary's second name was chosen in memory of her grandmother. That is a constant reminder to me of my mother, a woman of faith whose beauty and grace adorned our home and made it such a welcoming place. That memory has been an inspiration to me as we have been led to open our home to the refugees who became our extended family.

As I look back I can say with assurance that God has been utterly faithful. In good times and in bad we have found him true to his promise to be with us, and in his presence there is love and care and total security.

EPILOGUE

There is an urgent need in the western world, where unbelief is rampant, where moral standards have plummeted, and where many who once showed interest in the Christian faith have given it up or been lulled to sleep by our materialistic society, to live lives consecrated to the Master's service. I have witnessed such consecration in the lives of God's servants in Southeast Asia as they work in searing heat and choking dust with only the basic necessities of life, and none of the luxuries we take for granted. They have a joy and contentment that is lacking here.

Christians in the Far East labour night and day in God's service, often for very little financial reward. Are they not worthy of their hire? (see Luke 10:7). We may not be called to overseas work, but we can support with our finance and prayer those who are. 'The harvest is plentiful, but the workers are few. Ask the Lord of the harvest, therefore, to send out workers into his harvest field' (Luke 10:2). But can we ask the Lord to do this if we are unprepared to support the people he sends, or those others, such as my friends in the Far East, who labour unstintingly in his harvest fields?

Jesus said, 'As long as it is day, I must do

the work of him who sent me. Night is coming, when no-one can work' (John 9:4). There is still time to carry out the Great Commission and spread the gospel. But time is running out and terrible judgements will yet fall on those who reject Christ. In this day of grace there are many who still have never heard the gospel message. Is our response to the Lord's command to do everything in our power to tell them? It won't be easy, wherever and however we are called to serve. God does not promise ease in his service. 'If anyone would come after me, he must deny himself and take up his cross daily and follow me' (Luke 9:23).

That deep red cross I saw in Vietnam, red with the blood of Jesus who gave himself for his people, still hangs in the dark skies of apostasy that threaten this land. It calls us to follow the risen Christ in a world where he is still rejected, and to display his love in lives that are dedicated to his service. And it still hangs in the dark skies of Communism and heathenism, challenging us to meet the spiritual and physical needs of unbelievers there, and to care for our brothers and sisters in those lands where to walk with him really does mean the way of the cross.

The great apostle Paul wrote to the Philippians from a dank, dark prison where he was held in chains. He said, 'Whatever was to my profit I now consider loss for the sake of Christ. What is more, I consider everything a loss compared to the surpassing greatness of knowing Christ Jesus my Lord, for whose sake I have lost all things. I consider them rubbish, that I may gain Christ and be found in him, not having a righteousness of my own that comes from the law, but that which is through faith in Christ – the righteousness that comes from God and is by faith. I want to know Christ and the power of his resurrection and the fellowship of sharing in his sufferings, becoming like him in his death, and so, somehow, to attain to the resurrection from the dead' (Philippians 3:7-11).

What a wonderful example Paul is of a man whose life was spent in service to the risen Lord! But Paul's service cost him years in prison and a martyr's death, a price he counted gain, not loss. He knew that before him lay the prize of the crown of righteousness. In our materialistic society we lose sight of eternal values and are in danger of being neither hot nor cold, just like the Laodicean church in the book of Revelation. May we shake off our lethargy and seek some service for Christ through which we can win souls, minister to the needy, help the weak and homeless and build up the church in these last days.

A new day will shortly dawn when the time for seeing souls saved will have gone forever. Then we shall behold Jesus face to face in glory in that holy city, the New Jerusalem. There the refugee, redeemed by the blood of Jesus, will find an eternal home in which he is for ever safe and secure; those who have suffered for the sake of the gospel will wear crowns of life; and wars, famine and death will have gone for ever.

'No longer will there be any curse. The throne of God and of the Lamb will be in the city, and his servants will serve him. They will see his face, and his name will be on their foreheads. There will be no more night. They will not need the light of a lamp or the light of the sun, for the Lord God will give them light. And they will reign for ever and ever' (Rev 22:3-5).

The New Millennium for Cambodia[1]

As I write this it is Prachum Ben here in Cambodia, a time when the people rush to different Buddhist temples, taking food sacrifices to appease the souls or ghosts of their ancestors. For a week, so they believe, the gates of hell are opened, all nineteen different levels of hell disgorge the tortured souls of the ancestors and they are free to roam the land in search of food offerings. Unfaithful people, or families that do not provide food, are cursed by these spirits for the whole year to come. Such is the spiritual bondage in this poverty stricken country where there is a massive level of malnutrition that, caught in a cycle of fear and appeasement to a host of spirits and powers, food is still offered year by year.

Cambodia is a beautiful country and her people rich in hospitality. But, beneath the quick and genuine smiles and the tranquil rural scenery, there is a deeply scarred and hurt nation. The past thirty years of war, genocide and betrayal has brought this small land to its knees. Pol Pot's legacy from his four years of destruction that was the Killing Fields left a quarter of the

---

1. Contributed by Nigel Goddard, Executive Director, Southeast Asian Outreach Cambodia, PO Box 85, Phnom Penh, Cambodia.

population dead, including the educated: doctors, teachers and others with professional skills were systematically executed, and the infrastructure of the country was destroyed. Trust, hope and social cohesion were erased.

Yet, in this ravaged country, poverty, malnutrition and land mines are not the only reality. The message of this book is a witness and testimony of hope. The message of the cross is one of redemption and renewal. God is at work today, using his people to touch individuals even in the darkest and most oppressive situations. God's compassion is at work. The past that was the Killing Fields is being replaced by a future with the potential to be harvest fields.

Brenda describes her second visit in 1993, when the United Nations had a huge peace keeping military presence in Cambodia supervising the democratic election that paved the way for full international recognition. That marked a significant step up in the level of international assistance that is helping to rebuild the country. Southeast Asian Outreach (SAO) had been present in the country for two years by that time, the first exploratory visit coinciding with the weekend that the Vietnamese troops, which had ousted the Khmer Rouge over a decade earlier, withdrew from Cambodia.

Since then God's faithfulness and redemption in individual lives has been mirrored in the life of the nation. The 1990s have seen growth in the church by more than fortyfold. The Khmer Rouge threat, still destabilising the country in 1993, is now history and its leaders face trial. Cambodia, the newest member of ASEAN, looks ahead to political stability and growth. Not even the evils of the Khmer Rouge are beyond the power and grace of God. Duch, the infamous head of the Khmer Rouge secret police and Chief of Toul Sleng Death Camp, who is awaiting trial, has become a Christian, the only Khmer Rouge leader to fully confess and accept his crimes, saying, 'Now my future is in God's hands.' Cambodia is a signatory of the Ottawa Mine Ban Treaty and faces the real and growing prospect of peace.

And yet

The needs and hurts remain huge in this, one of the poorest countries in Asia, with a GDP of less than $200 per year, with an imminent HIV/AIDS epidemic of alarming proportions, where 49% of children under the age of five are either moderately or severely underweight, and where 40% of the rural population is below the poverty line. Of one thousand children entering grade one at school, only twenty will graduate from secondary school. The road ahead is still long, steep and pot-holed. That is why this book is so powerful. It reminds us to look above and beyond the immediate situation. God's power and touch upon lives, bringing joy and peace from hopeless and tragic situations, is an inspiring witness.

SAO Cambodia stands with the testimony of this book. God is indeed active. Hope is real and Cambodians, one life at a time, are experiencing God's love, mercy and power. As his people share their lives, live out and speak the gospel and work through the multitude of needs that poverty, marginalisation and vulnerability bring, the hope and transformation this book describes is multiplied. The SAO Cambodia projects described in Brenda's account are ongoing. All of them have now achieved, or are at the last stages of achieving, full Cambodian management, support and ownership. Helping poor subsistence farmers to provide protein foods for their families through farming fish, Khmer language tuition to allow expatriates to optimise their input, income generation through craft production, eye health care screening and services through optometry clinics, these all touch lives and are a witness to God's love expressed through his people.

As SAO Cambodia brings the incarnate Word to a hurting people, and follows Jesus' example of active, compassionate involvement, of empowering disciples and seeing their ministry multiply, we look ahead to developing new initiatives that will continue the process of rebuilding the country. Community development, community managed health, credit and income generation schemes, training, love, tears, prayer and commitment all work together in the Lord's service.

God's Word challenges each one of us, as does Brenda's book and the needs that surround us in this needy and lost world. How can I be involved? What should I pray? What should I give? How can I be a part of something that will change lives – mine included? The price may be high. Commitment, tears and discipleship do not come easy. But the prize, both now and in eternity, is absolutely guaranteed. Are you ready to make a difference? Are you ready to be used by God?

Christian Focus Publications publishes biblically-accurate books for adults and children. The books in the adult range are published in three imprints.

Christian Heritage contains classic writings from the past.

Christian Focus contains popular works including biographies, commentaries, doctrine, and Christian living.

Mentor focuses on books written at a level suitable for Bible College and seminary students, pastors, and others; the imprint includes commentaries, doctrinal studies, examination of current issues, and church history.

For a free catalogue of all our titles, please write to
Christian Focus Publications,
Geanies House, Fearn,
Ross-shire, IV20 1TW, Great Britain

For details of our titles visit us on our web site
http://www.christianfocus.com